The COLLECT'D WRIT~ INGS *of* Sᴛ. HERETICUS

The
COLLECT'D WRIT
INGS *of* Sᴛ. HERETICUS

Including Manuſcripts
that have not PREVIOUSLY *Appear'd in Print*
to which are *Annex'd* TWO APPENDIXES

ON

THEOLOGICAL GAMEſMANſHIP
& ONE ON

REſEARCHMANſHIP

For all of which the neceſſary editing has been
done, together with an Iɴᴛʀᴏᴅᴜᴄᴛɪᴏɴ,

BY

Robert McAfee Brown

Monotyp'd for THE WEſTMINſTER PREſS
PHILADELPHIA, PENNſYLVANIA
Aɴɴᴏ Dᴏᴍɪɴɪ 1964

LIBRARY OF CONGRESS CATALOG CARD NO. 64-14085

PRINTED IN THE UNITED STATES OF AMERICA

Published by The Westminster Press ®
Philadelphia, Pennsylvania

Dedicat'd to my dear friends

O. FELIX CULPA

&

MEA CULPA

without whose existence these pages

would have been neither possible

nor neceſſary

"The memory of them will long be sweet"
— C. FALLOR SUM, as cited on a
Kinkardineshire tombstone

Acknowledgments

M ost of the material in the following pages originally appeared in *Christianity and Crisis*. The editors have kindly consented to its reappearance in the present form and to the use of the drawing of St. Hereticus by June Goldsborough, on which is based the jacket design for this book. "What's Where in Barth," however, was first published in *The Christian Century*, while the two appendixes on "Theological Gamesmanship" first appeared in *Religion in Life*, under the pseudonym of the editor. A number of the pieces, including the "Introduction" and "Theological Researchmanship" appear here in print for the first time.

CONTENTS

❧

PART TWO

The World's Important Religions
(A Series)

PART THREE

Making the Bible Relevant:
Biblical Needs and How to Meet Them

Appendixes

The COLLECT'D WRIT~
INGS *of* Sᴛ. HERETICUS

INTRODUCTION

By the Editor

IT WAS A MATTER of no little surprise to the present writer, when he began his graduate research some years ago, to discover that there no longer exists a reliable life of St. Hereticus, and that the standard histories of dogma have accorded him little or no attention. Indeed, certain otherwise valuable works of theological scholarship fail even to mention his name.[1] It was to fulfill this lamentable lacuna in the history of scholarship that the present study was undertaken, and the results of the subsequent research have suggested that the author's findings may be of use to a wider range of readers than simply his original Ph. D. committee. Thus, although the pages that follow were originally prepared as a dissertation, they have been recast by the omission of much technical material in order that they may be more comprehensible to the average intelligent layman.

[1] Cf. *inter alia*, the following: Aquinas, T., *Summa Theologica* (24 vols.), and *Summa Contra Gentiles* (5 vols.), Bacon Press, Boston, 1867 (first edition), P. Blanshard, editor; Aquinas, Jerome F. X., O.S.B., *Zur Phänomenologie der Begegnung*, The Rationalist Press, London, 3d, post free; James, William, *Das Konzil von Trent über das Verhältnis der Heiligen Schrift und der nichtgeschreiben Tradition*, University of South Dakota Press, n.d.; Sartre, J.-P., *Qui êtes-vous? La question fondamentelle de l'être et le néant dans le XIXme siècle*, S.C.M. Press, Avenue de Louis Quatorze, Paris, Maine.

On the other hand, however, Denzinger, *Enchiridion Symbolorum, Definitionum et Declarationum de Rebus Fidei et Morum*, Herder, Barcelona, Editio 31 (K. Rahner, S.J., ed.), surely makes more than a veiled reference to St. Hereticus in paragraph 46.

It is not claimed that the definitive work on St. Hereticus is here being presented, but only that the subsequent pages can represent, as it were, a clearing of the ground, in which, if not all the answers to knotty problems have been offered, at least (so it can be hoped) the proper questions have been asked. The present writer asks no more for his modest researches than that future scholars, building upon these initial investigations, may be enabled thereby to uncover more material, so that the theological world will finally possess what it so richly deserves — a more adequate appraisal of the Saint's life and thought than is at present available.

I. Past Research

The standard lives of Hereticus have usually divided his life into three periods: the early period, the middle period, and the late period.[2] A slightly more prosaic, but (considering the time in which it was initially proposed) equally accurate, typology was developed by Murray Cardinal (Alfred E.) Newman, who rather daringly divided the periods of Hereticus' life in the following threefold fashion: (1) first period, (2) second period, and (3) third period.[3] This approach, although less imaginative than that of Goode, had the advantage, not unappreciated by subsequent generations of students, of being more easily remembered and thus providing a ready series of reference points with which to collate the various events of Hereticus'

---

[2] Cf. *inter alia*, E. Goode, *Überlieferungsgeschichte des Hereticus*, Band I, Vandenhoech, Ruprecht and O'Flaherty, Madrid, 1916.
[3] Cf. his *Überlieferungsgeschichte des Hereticus, Zweite (Shelburne Falls) Band*, Stuttgart, W. Kohlhammer, 1916–1944.

life, such as, for example, viz., e.g., his birth and death.[4]

On the other hand, the twofold typology of the Baptist scholar Dimmvitt (failed B. Litt., Oxon, 1741), dividing Hereticus' life into its (a) decline and (b) fall,[5] must surely be rejected as representing an ideological bias that later research has demonstrated to have run through all the writings of the otherwise renowned Latvian scholar.[6]

II. Suggestions for a New Typology

The most comprehensive way to interpret the richly varied events of Hereticus' life will be to employ a three-fold typology, following to this extent the framework of the early researches of Goode and Newman, but to break with the descriptive terms urged by them, and to propose a newer and more comprehensive synoptic schema. To do so is in no sense to cast the slightest shadow of aspersion upon the sincerity of these earlier scholars, who were doing the best they could with the (then) meager resources available in German. Nevertheless, the uncovering of recent evidence, particularly in the field of archaeology, suggests that to persist any longer in dividing the periods of Hereticus' life into either: (a) (1) early, (2) middle, and (3) late, or (b) (1) first, (2) second, and (3) third, is to be guilty of ignoring conclusive new evidence.

---

[4] Newman's typology suggests, therefore, that the birth would be located in the first (1st) period, whereas the death would be assigned to the third (3d). The other events of Hereticus' life, accordingly, belong within the second (2d) period, or the period referred to by Goode as *das Mittelpunkt*.

[5] Cf. his *The Decline and Fall of Heresy* [*sic!*], Cambridge University Press, Cambridge, Massachusetts, 1742.

[6] Dimmvitt, after being sent down from Oxford, matriculated at Cambridge, where he became an expert in Latvian folklore, flora, and fauna.

Accordingly, the typology that will be proposed and defended in the pages below divides Hereticus' life into the following three periods: (a) the period of imitation, (b) the period of experimentation, and (c) the period of creativity. It will immediately be seen how much richer and more pregnant with possibility is such a proposed typology, particularly when compared in detail, point by point, with the earlier and now to be discarded hypotheses of Goode and Newman; [7] and that in comparison to it the outlandish proposal of Dimmvitt [8] does not even bear mention in the same

paragraph.

III. The Archaeological Evidence

It has already been suggested that the fundamental reason for proposing a radically new typology as the basis for a fresh understanding of the life and thought of St. Hereticus is based on archaeological evidence only recently uncovered. Such is indeed the case, as those who have studied the caves near those in which the Dead Sea Scrolls were found will surely be among the first to admit. [9]

The new evidence, simply described, consists of a fragment of a jar, or sherd, found in the inner recesses of Cave LXX and therefore written in Greek, a reproduction of which is included in Figure I.

It seems not improbable to conjecture, in accordance with the brilliant researches of G. Urn Estreitt, that the

---

[7] *Vide supra*, p. 2.

[8] *Vide supra*, p. 3.

[9] Efforts are being made even now to get the following Old Testament scholars to make this admission: B. Anderson, W. F. Albright, J. Muilenburg, J. Bright, Fr. J. Fitzmyer, S.J., as well as Edmund Wilson, the Old Testament expert for *The New Yorker* magazine.

Figure 1

Fragment of a jar, or sherd, found in Cave
LXX, and therefore written in Greek, to which
reference is made in the text (see above).

stone out of which this sherd, or jar, was made is sodorifer-
ous calcifying limestone (*soderiferii calcificientibus lime-
stoneitis*), and that it therefore represents the earliest
extant reference to St. Hereticus. The latter supposition
is based upon a reconstruction of the missing portion of
the jar, or sherd, in a fashion illustrated in Figure 2, in

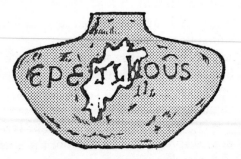

Figure 2

Reconstruction of the earliest extant reference
to St. Hereticus. (*Note:* the shaded portions
represent the conjectured reconstruction.)

which the shaded portions represent the conjectured reconstruction.

The archaic spelling ἐρέτικοῦς (or, as we would transliterate it, *Hereticous*) is accounted for by the brilliant conjecture of Schmerlhausen-Möllendorff, which would seem to indicate either (a) that the sherd, or jar, is even older than previously conjectured, or (b) that people didn't spell very well in those days. It might also indicate (c) that the conjecture is wrong.[10] The theory, at all events, is universally referred to by the Jerusalem Bedouins who haunt the marketplaces as "Schmerlhausen-Möllendorff's Omicron." The careful scholar who is disturbed by the presence of the (unnecessary) omicron will note, however, that it can be discarded without disturbing by so much as a shred the light shed upon the sherd.[11]

When all the available data concerning this jar fragment is accumulated in one place, the following information relative to a conjecture about the possible dates of Hereticus' life and influence may be taken into account:

    a. Cave LXX is at least as old as creation, but presumably not older.

    b. The dust in which the sherd was found comes from Sumerian vegetation, suggesting a violent earth upheaval, since Cave LXX is in Samaria rather than Sumeria.

    c. There is no evidence that the fall of Jericho (1347 B.C.) disturbed the location of the sherd in relation to other items in the cave.

---

[10] This is a possibility that did not occur to Schmerlhausen-Möllendorff.

[11] This possibility did not occur to Schmerlhausen-Möllendorff, either.

d. The calligraphy on the sherd is from the Golden Age of Greece, or is at least (so much R. Lynn admits) a very clever imitation of a writer of that time.

e. The sherd was discovered in Cave LXX in 1947 at about 4 P.M. on the afternoon of October 29, by a wandering Aramaean shepherd boy named Lightfoot.

f. In tiny letters on the reverse side of the sherd is inscribed the legend "Souvenir of Atlantic City."

On the basis of the above evidence, the terminal dates in either direction for dating the sherd (and thus casting valuable light upon the probable existence *at that time* of St. Hereticus) can be seen to be represented by items a and e which indicate, respectively, the dates 4004 B.C. and October A.D. 1947. It is not, of course, a foregone conclusion that Hereticus failed to flourish *beyond* either the *terminus ad quem* or the *terminus ad quo,* but the evidence makes clear that he flourished at least within the period comprised by the *terminus ad quem* and the *terminus ad quo,* cited above.[12]

---

[12] To put the same point in somewhat simpler language, Hereticus could have been alive *before* his name was inscribed on the jar, and he could also have been alive *after* his name was inscribed on the jar. Or, to posit the opposite conjecture, he could have been *dead* before his name was inscribed on the jar, and he could have been dead *after* his name was inscribed on the jar. Only two other possibilities remain, both of which have been advanced by R. Handy: (a) that he might have been dead *before* his name was inscribed on the jar *but not after*, or (b) that he might have been *alive* before his name was inscribed on the jar, but *not* after. But this is surely to quibble.

IV. THE HISTORICAL EVIDENCE

Part of the reason for the dearth of interpretive material about St. Hereticus can be attributed to the same factor that was responsible for the relative neglect of Søren Kierkegaard (1813–1855) until after the First World War, and a number of interesting historical parallels can be drawn between S. H. and S. K. Kierkegaard was neglected, of course, primarily because he wrote in a language not widely spoken or read in Europe save for a small area directly south of Kattegat and Skagerrak.[13] Kierkegaard was therefore overlooked until his works began to be translated into German.[14]

Similarly, the works of Hereticus were for many centuries denied a wide reading public due to general unfamiliarity with the tongue in which they were written. One of his earliest extant articles, for example, written somewhere toward the middle of the sixth century A.D.,[15] was incomprehensible to even the most learned scholars for nearly a millennium, since it was written in a twentieth-century English patois that was far from common even as late as 1955, the same year, interestingly enough, in

---

[13] Denmark.

[14] The preposterous theory that Walter Lowrie first translated Kierkegaard (hereafter referred to as S. K.) into German, and only later into English, in order to collect double royalties, is beneath contempt. W. J. Wolf, E.T.S., in a forthcoming work on S. K. (hereafter referred to as Kierkegaard) does not even bother to comment on this hypothesis, considering it to be the work of some "piddling pedant" (to borrow the Great Dane's pregnant phrase) with an anti-Anglican bias not shared by Wolf himself.

[15] Anheuser-Busch, in an unpublished monograph to which the present writer was privileged to have access whilst preparing the present introduction, has recently offered evidence suggesting that it may have been slightly *after* the middle of the sixth century A.D.

which the Brooklyn Dodgers first won a World Series.[16]

All of this suggests that from the point of view of historical research, the actual facts of the life of St. Hereticus are difficult to determine with certainty and scholarly objectivity. The absence from Herr F. Umlaut's monumental *Geschichte des Gottesglaubens und Abgottesglaubens* [17] of any reference to Hereticus is disappointing to expert and dilettante alike, as is the similarly total neglect accorded Hereticus in the exhaustive work of Monsieur J. Laplume de Matante, *L'histoire des herétiques*.[18]

It is noteworthy that Hertzmann, Ertzmann, Reitzmann, Eschermann, Tischermann, Irtzmann, Cook, Umbilicus, and even Seidenweinder, no matter what else they may have disagreed about, are at one in the indisputable fact that they accord *no place whatever in any of their writings* to the influences at work upon Hereticus in what we have chosen to call his "imitative" period.[19]

---

[16] Anheuser-Busch has insisted, in a second unpublished monograph to which the present writer was privileged to have access whilst preparing the present introduction, that the English patois in which Hereticus wrote was actually a part of the lingua franca of the American Midwest as early as 1920, the same year, interestingly enough, in which Bill Wambsganss of the Cleveland Indians made the first and thus far only unassisted triple play in World Series history. The repetition here of the Trinity-motif is surely more than sheer coincidence.

[17] Marburg, 1894, 7 vols.

[18] Paris and Barcelona, Rue Voltaire 94, 27 vols., 1909 ff.

[19] It is claimed by some, notably by Vater Baer in his *Pugilissimus Bellicosis*, that Hereticus himself was the author of the volumes attributed to the above-named scholars, and that natural modesty forbade his calling undue attention to his own work. Herr Baer's theory stands or falls on his ingenious discovery that the namesof the above authors form an acrostic of the word "Hereticus." An even fuller exposition of this position is contained in F. Baer, M. Baer, and B. Baer, *Bellicosis Pugilissimus*, in which the three Baers buttress the findings of Vater Baer. Charles Friedrich Ibid (1699–1703) (hereafter referred to as C. F. Ibid), however, disagrees with the evidence presented in the

Harnack, however, is an exception.[20] For as the learned church historian of the so-called nineteenth century so vividly and succinctly put it, "[Hereticus] is obviously . . . being referred to here."[21]

Rather significantly, this very line *and this line alone* (italics mine) has been omitted from the English translation of the *Dogmengeschichte*. It has been suggested elsewhere[22] that this curious omission (*vide infra*) is simply another link in the chain of evidence suggesting what the Scots call a *conspiratorio ex silentio*, but, *mutatis mutandis* and *ex post facto*, at least three other hypotheses have been advanced to account for this curious omission (*vide supra*), so little commented on by previous scholars.[23] These hypotheses, reduced to their bare essentials, can be stated as follows:

---

first of these two volumes and has published his findings in a learned monograph, *Nein, Herr Baer!* (E.T., *Ne'er Herr Baer!*) Berteschgarten, 1944, 8 vols., cxxvii + 12 pp., privately printed, claiming that the real author of the works attributed to Hertzmann, Ertzmann, Reitzmann, Eschermann, Tischermann, Irtzmann, Cook, Umbilicus, and Seidenweinder was an obscure French theologian of the post neo-Gallican school named Tishcurée. Interesting enough, Ibid bases *his* conjecture not on acrostical evidence but on anagramatical evidence, as meticulous scrutiny of the word "Tishcurée" will soon make apparent to the careful scholar.

[20] Cf. his *Allegemeine zu Festschrift für alles Vergessen Zubleichkeit*, hereafter cited as *Allegemeine z. Festschrift für alles Vergessen Zubleichkeit*.

[21] Harnack, Adolf von, *Dogmengeschichte* (E.T., *History of Dogma*), 7 vols., Vol. V, p. 714, my translation. The full quotation reads, "Eusebius is obviously not being referred to here." (*Sic*.)

[22] Cf. the writer's unpublished monograph. "Ellipses in Harnack," microfilm, Harvard Divinity School Library, 1926, submitted in partial fulfillment of the requirements for the degree of bachelor of divinity.

[23] Among the scholars who have not commented on the omission are, *inter alia*, Reinhold Niebuhr, Paul Tillich, Rudolf Bultmann, Martin Buber, Hans Küng, and H. Jackson Forstman.

a. That matters of personal taste intruded into the translator's otherwise impeccable objectivity, since his mother, by her own admission, "had been affrighted by an heretic two months before childbirth";

b. That the sentence was omitted at the publisher's insistence in order to save space;

c. That the translator was well within his rights in omitting the sentence, since it actually does not occur in the original German.

The authorities are fairly well divided on the relative value of these various conjectures,[24] though the present writer believes that a more plausible case can be made for option c than can as adequately be made, at least on the basis of presently available evidence, for either of the other two options, i.e., a or b, or even a combination of the two, e.g., a/b.[25]

One must conclude, indeed, that greater emphasis has been placed upon the Harnack reference than a serious examination of the material will warrant.[26] It will be

---

[24] Cf. the writer's unpublished monograph, "Further Light on Ellipses in Harnack," microfilm, Yale Divinity School Library, 1928, submitted in partial fulfillment of the requirements for the degree of bachelor of divinity.

[25] Cf. Ibid., *op. cit.*, lvii (June 31, 1907, pp. 21, 29, 67, 69, 84, 96, 121–123, 344–349, 718 *et seq.*, as well as the interesting, though palpably implausible conjecture of the Italian existentialist, Salvatore Ambulando, in his *Existential Schizophrenia* (E.T., *Schizophrenic Existentialism, or Either/Or and/or Both/And*), Vol. II, Florence, Ponte Vecchio 9, pp. 21–16, 147–121, and the 39 articles that comprise the Table of Contents. The latter, of course, are not doctrinally binding in Great Britain.

[26] Cf. the writer's unpublished monograph, "Harnackian Elliptical Constructions in the Light of Recent Research," microfilm, Library of the Iliff School of Theology, 1930, submitted in partial fulfillment of the requirements for the degree of bachelor of divinity.

necessary, therefore, to turn to other sources than the otherwise reliable *Dogmengeschichte* (E.T., *History of Dogma*) if the careful scholar is to reconstruct with accuracy and scholarly precision the events of Hereticus' life and influence.[27]

It is possible to summarize briefly the available evidence from other, non-Harnackian sources in terms of the following six propositions:

1. It appears that St. Hereticus was born about A.D. 10, so that his mature years, and the beginning of his major influence, are seen to coincide roughly with the beginning of the Christian era.[28]

2. In their jointly edited work, both J. Christiaan Smorgasbord, of Utrecht, and Mortimer A. Phlym-Phlam, the British Unitarian dogmatist, credit St. Hereticus with playing a decisive, indeed *the* decisive, role in the composition of the Nicene Creed.[29]

3. Dr. Dmitri ("Mitya") Doppeloppeloppelopovitch, A.B., B.D., M.A., Ph.D., D.D., Litt.D., D. Phil.,

---

[27] Cf. the writer's unpublished monograph, "Ellipses in Harnack? The Discovery of a Theological *Cul-de-Sac*," microfilm, Union Theological Seminary Library, 1932, submitted in partial fulfillment of the requirements for the degree of bachelor of divinity.

[28] Cf. M. O. James, *The Apocryphal New Testament*, O.U.P. (o.p.), for a collection of examples of Hereticus' early works, all of them appearing under the guise of pseudonyms. Although these early examples are stylistically crude, they have a certain daring and *flair*, as the French would say, which makes plain, even at this early date, that their author will one day become a man with whom theology must reckon. J. Porter, the great Maurice expert, has made this clear.

[29] Cf. their *The Decline of Truth: A Study of the Transition from Ethics to Chalcedonianism*, The Constantinian Press, A.D. 461, esp. p. 325.

et seq., who has won justly deserved fame as an interpreter of Eastern Orthodoxy with his *The Parting of East and West* (E.T., *East of the Sun and West of the Moon*), says only of Hereticus and his son (*Heretico filioque*), "*fl. ca.* A.D. 1054."

4. A Counter-Reformation document [30] states positively that St. Hereticus attained the height of his influence on October 31, 1517, and concludes with the statement that among Protestants his doctrines have been believed "everywhere, always, and by all" (*quod ubique, quod semper, quod ab omnibus*).

5. Certain Reformation writers [31] place the major activities of St. Hereticus several decades, and even centuries, earlier than the Tridentine authors referred to in point 4 (four) above. These authors claim that Hereticus [32] was most obviously active during the late medieval and early Renaissance period, particularly in an urban area centering about halfway up [33] the west coast of the Italian peninsula.[34]

---

[30] Cited in studies by "Flick, Spiazzi, Rambaldi, Bea, Batic, Filograssi, Dhanis, and Boyer" (cf. K. Rahner, *Theological Investigations*, Larton, Dongman, and Todd, p. 40).

[31] Cf. *inter alia*, Luther, Martin; Zwingli, Huldreich; Calvin, John; Melanchthon, Philipp; Knox, John; Bucer, Martin; *omnia opera*.

[32] Significantly, the title "St." is not used.

[33] Some authorities claim the location to be about halfway *down*.

[34] J. Barr, however (not to be confused with J. Baer, *vide supra*), is inclined to place the center of influence in contemporary Germany; one receives the impression from his writings that most of the articles in the multivolumed *Theologisches Wörterbuch zum Neuen Testament* were actually written by Hereticus, even though they appear under pseudonyms that closely resemble the names of some of Europe's most distinguished scholars and theologians.

6. The most important fact of all is that no account of St. Hereticus makes any direct mention of his death.[35] Even more important is the fact that St. Hereticus is one of the very few saints for whom no authenticated relics have been discovered. The reader, however, must not jump to hasty conclusions concerning the meaning of this latter piece of evidence. It will be noted that the statement refers (a) to *authenticated* relics, which (b) have not *yet* been discovered. It is always, of course, possible that Old Testament archaeological expeditions will uncover new evidence.[36]

V. Conclusions

What are we to conclude from this richly documented testimony, reached, as it has been, quite apart from any direct dependence on the recent researches of Geiselmann, Lengsfeld, and O'Hanlon, which were published too late to be incorporated into the present survey?

An impartial weighing of the testimony leads to the tentative suggestion that St. Hereticus may still be alive.

---

[35] But *vide supra*, p. 3, in which reference is made to Newman's citing of the death (*sic*) of Hereticus as an example of an event to be located within the third (3d) period of Hereticus' life. Aside from the obvious semantic problem of justifying the inclusion of the event of "death" *within* the event of "life" ("death" and "life" being, from a strictly logical and semantic point of view, mutually exclusive concepts), it should be borne in mind that nowhere does Newman actually give any *specific* data about the events surrounding what we are only entitled to refer to as the "alleged death" of St. Hereticus. It is clear, therefore, that Newman's reference to death (*mors, mortis, f.*) is of an illustrative, rather than of a substantive, nature.

[36] *Vide supra*, pp. 4–7, for a review of the present state of archaeological evidence on this matter.

At the very least, if he himself has not survived the ages, he has clearly bequeathed to subsequent generations such a multitude of progeny (*Hereticus filiique*), each equipped with a fecundity no less astonishing than his own, that those principles to which St. Hereticus dedicated himself, summarized in his own pregnant utterance, *De gustibus non disputandum*, have clearly found their own exponents in every age.

Does this mean, then, that the quest of the historical Hereticus has been in vain? Not at all. It has suggested very clearly, however, the need for a *new* quest of the historical Hereticus, a task that may well be as important to some future theological generation, as was the task of demythologizing St. Nicholas to a preceding one.[37]

A final question remains. Why has the church seen fit to canonize this errant son of hers, whose life appears to have been dedicated to confusing the faith, confounding the faithful, and comforting the faithless? The truth of the matter is very simple. Mother Church, in her infinite wisdom, would prefer heresy to flourish within her walls, where she can keep track of it, rather than to have it rampant in attack upon her from without. She recognizes, furthermore, that the heretic is not totally wrong, and that his sin consists not so much in a flagrant denial of the truth as in an overemphasis on one aspect of the truth, in such a way as to distort it but not totally destroy it.

Thus St. Hereticus (for it is indeed from him that the cognate employed in the above paragraph has been de-

---

[37] Cf. the work of the eminent Anglican divine, the Rev. Clement Moore, of General Theological Seminary, New York City, U.S.A., *Nox ante Christmissam erat.*

rived) plays a significant role in the ongoing life of the church, a role that it has been the purpose of these pages to suggest, however briefly; and his utterances can be beneficial to all believers who are prepared to see the grain of truth enshrined in them, at the same time that they resist the temptation to follow him all the way down a road that is paved with good intentions.

Robert McAfee Brown

Crow's Nest
Windrush
Lade Braes
St. Andrews
Fife
Scotland
U.K.
N.A.T.O.
April 1, 1964 (the Feast of St. Hereticus)

PART ONE

Words of Cheer for the Local Church

◈

UNDOING THE PASTOR'S WORK — I

IT HAS BEEN my discovery that almost all modern devices and inventions can be employed to keep the church on the side of heresy, and to prevent any warm embrace of the orthodox faith, no matter how hard the pastor may try to employ them to the latter end. I recall, for example, the use we made in Germany of the newly invented printing press back in the 1520's to publicize Brother Martin's tracts (although he, alas, was not nearly as heretical as I had at first supposed), not to mention the way modern television can be employed to bring all sorts of heresy within the reach of every full-blooded American who is too lazy to go to contemporary American churches and get it at first hand.

Television, however, is too obviously a means of compounding heresy to need my attention at the moment. I am thinking, rather, of that much more innocent and subtle tool of heresy, that junior cousin to television, the Kodachrome slide. The pastor who purchases a projector, screen, and camera for his church will think that he has hold of A Good Thing here, and so he has — but I have discovered that even the most dedicated efforts of the most dedicated pastor can easily be dispelled by a determined woman's group, or even by a determined woman.

Perhaps two case studies (you can see that I have been exposing myself to modern sociology) will show how the pastor's efforts in this area can be easily overcome.

CASE A: The pastor has gotten slide equipment in order to give illustrated lectures on the life of St. Paul or on modern church architecture. But what does the Woman's Group do? It asks the pastor, who is something of an amateur photographer himself, to give an illustrated lecture on "My Vacation Trip Through the Dakotas." Now it so happens that the pastor *does* have on hand 142 pictures (two were overexposed) of said trip that he took three summers ago, including a number of impressive shots of cloud formations. But he is much more eager to lecture on "Palestine: 1963," having likewise taken his camera there on a seventeen-day sponsored tour just a few months previous.

At this point, one of two things happens: (1) He may succumb to the pressures of the Woman's Group ("But, Reverend, we want to get to know you as a *person!*")

and show the slides of the Dakotas, salving his conscience by remembering that there *is* one blurred shot of a national missions station, taken by his wife through the windshield of their moving car on a rainy afternoon. In this case we need not worry. The day is won as surely as though the recording secretary of the Men's Brotherhood had shown his slides on "Trout Fishing in the Appalachians." (2) Or, on the other hand, the minister may prevail on the women to have a meeting on A Significant Topic, and show his pictures on "Palestine: 1963."

The latter course would appear to represent a clear victory for the well-intentioned pastor. He not only shows pictures of some of the traditional Christian sites (which as a matter of fact he has been verbally describing in every sermon since his return), but he also outlines in rather moving fashion the nature of the Arab-Israeli tensions and ends with a real plea for concern.

But it is still possible for the ladies to win the day — and on the basis of my observations I would assert that they usually do. They do it by taking the "ample time provided for questions" and using this time to propound variations of the following:

1. "Is there a good American hotel in Jericho?"
2. "Wasn't it frightfully hot?"
3. "Did you have good accommodations on the plane going over?"

Now, no pastor, not even one endowed with a considerable number of supernatural virtues, can emerge from this kind of barrage without feeling that he has met his match, and that his most dedicated efforts to make A Good Thing out of the meeting have somehow backfired.

His attempt to make the group socially conscious has led to nothing more than a series of pleasant and inconsequential trivialities.

CASE B: The use of Kodachrome slides as a way of Keeping The Young People also offers many diverting ways of avoiding coming to grips with the faith. All that is required is someone of slightly heretical leanings to operate the projector.

Thus when Paul is making his dramatic appeal before Festus, loud guffaws can be produced, rather than hushed appreciation, by having the slide projected upside down. Paul, standing on his head, is simply not, by anyone's standards, a dignified and impressive sight. The shipwreck scene, inserted sideways, can produce much the same effect.

A couple of such happenings, delicately spaced throughout the evening, with perhaps the inevitable map of Paul's three missionary journeys shown top for bottom, can ruin the point of a set of slides and completely twist the significance of the last lines of the script, which announce that the pictures have been an attempt to show that the early Christians were "the upsetters of the world."

UNDOING THE PASTOR'S WORK — II

MY DESIRE has always been to promote gentle heresy. The heresy must not be extreme or it will be detected and perhaps cast out. One of the most effective ways of achieving this end is to concentrate on the minister himself, particularly if he is one who appears to make orthodoxy interesting and even relevant. Consider, then, the following tried and true ways of exploiting the minister, so that he becomes less and less able to proclaim the gospel.

1. The first way is to deny the priesthood of all believers and promote the heresy that everything in the life of the church depends on the minister himself. The seeds can be planted just before a new minister arrives at a church. A few conversations opened with the words, "When the new minister comes . . ." can lead to the impression that certainly within a month of his arrival:

    a. Sunday school attendance will double.
    b. Giving will treble.
    c. Not only will there be two services on Sunday morning, but the sanctuary will have to be enlarged to accommodate the crowds.
    d. The bulletin will be printed on glossy paper instead of being mimeographed on the back side of those colored pictures in such ghastly good taste that come from a religious supply house.

When the new minister does come, of course, none of these things will happen, or if they do, they will happen only very slowly. The people are then able to blame the minister because he is not the sort of spiritual Superman they had expected. More significantly, they can avoid the obvious conclusion that these things are *their* responsibility as well, and perhaps avoid forever the less obvious (but more important) conclusion that these things are not really very important things in the life of the church. What more appealing heresy could there be than one that says that the church is not really the church unless it is a constantly buzzing hive of feverish activity, of many groups so busy being active that none of them is ever quite sure what the purpose of the activity is, and all of them much too busy ever to stop long enough to reflect upon the words, "Be still, and know that I am God"? Gifted indeed is the minister who can counter this — so gifted, indeed, that he will probably soon be called to "a field of wider service" (a phrase of my own invention).

2. A second way to undo the pastor's work is to insist that his pastoral activities be measured on an efficiency basis. Let us say that the minister takes his pastoral calling seriously. He is not one of these in-and-out-in-five-minutes-How's-the-family?-Why-wasn't-your-husband-in-church-last-Sunday?-Got-to-run-along-now-See-you-in-church-next-Sunday-*with*-your-husband-hearty-chuckle sort of pastors. No, he tries to get well acquainted, to build up a relationship not only for the present moment but for that day when he may have to enter the household in time of real need or tragedy, to pray, and even on occasion to bring the Sacrament to the bedside.

But these things all take time. And they have the frightening possibility of deepening the faith of all concerned. Therefore, the efficient promoter of heresy can undo all this work simply by a well-timed complaint at the Ladies' Aid or the Men's Fellowship: "What does that pastor of ours *do* all the time? Doesn't he *ever* go calling? Does he just *sit* in his office all day? Or go out and play golf? (I'm almost *positive* I saw him on the golf course three Mondays ago.) Why, he hasn't been to call in our home for *six months!*"

Chances are that the majority of any given church group will be able to say the same thing, and concur with emphasis on the "six months" bit. (The fact that there are 956 members in the church, and only one pastor, is an irrelevant consideration.) Thus the heretic has helpfully exploited the notion that the minister isn't really busy enough or that he doesn't seem to get any calling done. In this way an atmosphere of thinly veiled suspicion and distrust can be created, and to break his way through this will require so much of the pastor's effort that there will be little time left for the gospel to be heard or appropriated.

3. Finally, my brethren (appeals for heresy should be couched in as orthodox terminology as possible), there can be subtle attempts not only to undo the pastor's work, but (putting it most unsubtly) to undo the pastor. The most efficient method is surely flattery. A politician, I have discovered, always has enemies to keep him humble. But a minister! He can always be told how "wonderful" he is, how "helpful," how "necessary," how "good with the young people," how much his sermons are "enjoyed." And the gradual multiplication of such comments by the lovers of heresy is guaranteed to unhinge the humility of even the most dedicated servant of God.

Sometimes it is enough merely to stop referring to Trinity Methodist Church and begin referring to Rev. Mr. Blank's Church. This will reap subtle results of a most rewarding sort. And if, in addition, a few people begin to talk about going on Sunday mornings not to worship God but, rather, "to hear Mr. Blank preach," then conditions will be created in which heresy can grow quietly and unobtrusively until it quite chokes out any real belief.

The moment of victory will be signalized on that Sunday when the Rev. Mr. Blank begins a sermon illustration with the words, "A woman came into my study last week . . ." and goes on to show *not* how the power of the gospel saved her but how frightfully clever the Rev. Mr. Blank was in diagnosing her problem and providing her with a ready-made solution of his own.

THE CHURCHMAN'S COLORING BOOK

W E ARE MOVING from the era of the printed word (books) to the era of the printed picture (*Life, Look,* and *Bible Comics*), and from the era of the spoken word (radio and H. V. Kaltenborn) to the era of the spoken picture (TV and Bugs Bunny). This move has been reinforced by the emergence of coloring books for adults. There have been coloring books for executives, doctors, politicians, and right-wingers.

Surely the church must invade this field. Can we not ask some enterprising Methodist concern to offer us *The Nonsmokers' Coloring Book* or an anonymous author to give us *The Vatican Council Coloring Book*, in which the good guys and bad guys will be distinguished by the color of their hats?

But these are distant hopes. In the meantime, "The Churchman's Coloring Book" is offered to Initiate A Trend.

> INSTRUCTIONS: Some coloring books provide the pictures so that all you can do is to color them. But in this book you draw the pictures too, and make them fit the descriptions. Then you color them. In that order.

I am General Revelation.

I am under a cloud these days.

Color the cloud gray.

Some people say I have already disappeared
   from the theological scene.

But, like other Generals, I shall return.

I am a denominational executive.

I work in a big building.

Color my suit gray to show that I'm not too radical.

Color my tie red to show that I'm not too conservative.

People under me think I'm too autocratic.

People over me think I'm not forceful enough.

It's quite a bind.

I am a pastor in the Inner City.

Color me so that I am identified with my environment.

The Inner City is the real firing line of contemporary Protestantism.

We've got to minister to people where they are.

People are in the Inner City.

That's why I'm here.

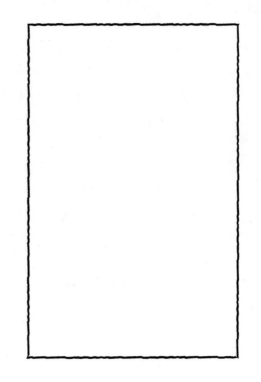

I am a pastor in Suburbia.

Color me so that I am identified with my environment.

Suburbia is the real firing line of contemporary Protestantism.

We've got to minister to people where they are.

People are in Suburbia.

That's why I'm here.

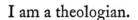

I am a theologian.

People say I live in a tower.

Color the tower ivory.

When I talk about the world, people say,
   " What do *you* know about the world? "

When I talk about theology, people say,
   " Why can't you be *relevant?* "

When I try to relate the two, people say,
   " Everybody's got to *specialize* these days."

It's quite a bind.

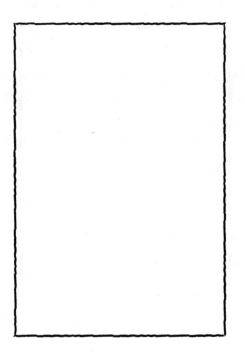

I'm just a humble Christian.

Cover me with sackcloth and ashes.

I'm not very good, but at least I know I'm
not very good.

I'm not very smart, but at least I know I'm
not very smart.

Other people may be better.

Other people may be smarter.

But at humility I can beat them all.

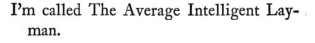

I'm called The Average Intelligent Layman.

Everybody writes books for me.

Everybody says I'm the one the church must reach.

Everybody says the future of Protestantism lies in my hands. Wow!

I blush to say that I can't understand the books.

Color me red.

I blanch when I admit that the church isn't reaching me.

Color me white.

I'm depressed about the future of Protestantism.

Color me blue.

I'm called The Average Intelligent Layman.

Color me red, white, and blue.

NOTES FOR THE SS SQUAD

S UNDAY SCHOOL manuals usually contain not only teaching suggestions and playtime activities but also helpful comments for teachers who have to cope with "difficult" pupils.

I humbly suggest that "difficult" pupils aren't the problem at all. The real dilemma of the modern Sunday School is just the reverse: how to cope with the "difficult" teacher. Herewith, therefore, a brief manual of arms for the SS Squad — the kids — on how to deal with different types of difficult teachers.

1. *The-teacher-who-is-an-obvious-attention-getter.* Nearly every class will have at least one teacher who wants attention and tries to dominate the group. Be sympathetic with him, and realize that he probably comes from a difficult home situation. Perhaps you can call on him during the week and come to understand his problem at its source.

There comes a time, however, when you must let him know who's really in charge. Draw the line if he tries to get cheap laughs, as many teachers do, by the annoying habit of insisting on the use of Christian names. You can be sure that he is insecure and playing to the gallery if he persists in referring to Spike as "Frederick," or looks in the direction of Butch and calls him "William."

2. *The teacher-who-isn't-prepared.* There will be days when you will enter the Sunday School classroom and discover that your teacher hasn't done his assignment.

Here are some giveaway signs: (a) feverish glances at the lesson manual while you are entering; (b) circles under the eyes; (c) periodic yawning; (d) an excessive amount of time spent on the preliminaries, such as taking attendance, distributing Bibles, inquiring in detail about those who are absent; (e) secret glances at his watch, about every 45 seconds, to see if dismissal time has come; and (f) a suggestion offered rather vaguely but at great length, that "pretty soon we ought to start thinking about the possibility of a Saturday hike when the weather begins to look good again." The clincher, however, will be if he lets you *keep* talking about yesterday's football game and finally joins in the discussion himself.

The teacher must not, of course, be allowed to get away with such faking maneuvers to cover up his unpreparedness. This would be Detrimental To His Growth. The best way to teach him how costly such unpreparedness can be is very simple: ask him, with relentless intensity, questions about the lesson. Glance at your manual (one page *beyond* where he had to stop when you came in the door) and ask him loudly, so all can hear, "Sir, just who *was* Ahijah?" or, "What does it mean here about the sin against the Holy Ghost?"

Note carefully that the question must be what we call a "Content Question" and not a "Thought Question." Thought Questions make it possible for the teacher to bluff by rambling (i.e., thinking). If the teacher fortifies his attempted response by a hasty glance at the manual, comment when he finishes, "Oh, but it says all *that* in the manual."

3. *The teacher-who-breaks-up-fights.* Almost every Sunday School will have a teacher who seems to come there with the sole purpose of breaking up fights. Whenever a

fight is in progress, you can be sure that he will be in the middle of it, trying to stop it.

But Sunday School fights are very important. Where, after all, can one better prepare for the church fights in which one will engage as an adult than at Sunday School? Sunday School fights, therefore, must be promoted, and the best way is to try to interest the teacher in the very activity he is attempting to stifle, so that he can become a part of the group instead of remaining an outsider. If, for example, the two or more contestants will forget about their animosities against one another long enough to team up against the interfering teacher, they will discover that sometimes the incurring of physical violence upon his person, perhaps in the neighborhood of the shin, can cause him to lose his temper and enter into the fray more uninhibitedly. Then what fun and games are in store for all!

Note: The principle here described can also be used for a variant of the above type, namely, *the-teacher-who-confiscates-peashooters.* However, if physical violence does not produce the desired end, try to interest the teacher in the educational values of the peashooter. What an exciting way, for example, to teach Palestinian geography: stand ten feet from a wall map, line everybody up, and see who can come closest to hitting Jerusalem smack in the middle. Best two out of three wins.

4. *The - teacher - who - promises - a - Saturday - party - " if-you're-all-good."* This is a kind of desperate last-ditch stand to which some teachers will resort in an effort to win popularity. It must not, of course, be tolerated. If it is, the teacher will get the impression that he can buy your attention. The most effective, though not necessarily the most kind, reprisal is to be perfectly angelic during

the trial period, and then (if I may employ a theological expression) raise hell at the party.

This will put an end to all future bargaining and bartering for good conduct and leave the teacher squarely faced with the problem of making the class interesting enough so that a certain amount of good conduct will result without your even being aware of it. Nothing worse for a teacher than letting you be aware that you're "being good." Brings original sin right to the surface.

"AFTER PRAYERFUL CONSIDERATION" — AN ALL-PURPOSE CHURCH REPORT FORM

ONCE a year all over the country the assembly halls groan from the accumulated weight of denominational gatherings. The various groups get together to review the year's work, congratulate themselves on their achievements, and disperse to harvest new achievements to report the following year. The one real fly in this ecclesiastical ointment is that the delegates have to give an accounting when they get home. The following all-purpose report form is offered to make their task easier:

A Report on the (*Annual, Semiannual, Quarterly*) Denominational (*Meeting, Assembly, Conference*)

INSTRUCTIONS: Underline (*at will, with caprice, after prayerful consideration*) the words in parentheses that are most descriptive of the meetings you attended, and read to your (*Men's Club, Women's Club, Thursday Circle*).

Seldom (*in the history of our denomination, if ever, in the past*) has one been as conscious of (*the power of the Holy Spirit, the strength of our denomination, the foresight of our denominational executives*) as at our recent (*assembly, meeting, conference*). From the first session to the last, as we came together (*to discuss, to chart, to prayerfully consider* [1]) our task for the future, it was clear that we were being guided by (*a Power outside ourselves, the guidance of the Holy Spirit, the wise planning of our denominational executives*) and being (*led, empowered, helped*) to see how we should (*plot our course, do God's will, revise the budget*) to meet the great demands that (*the present emergency, the challenge of mass communications, God*) places upon us.

Nowhere was (*the power of the Holy Spirit, the strength of our denomination, the foresight of our denominational executives*) more clearly evidenced than in the selection of our new (*moderator, chairman, executive secretary*). (*Mr., Dr., Rev.*) Blank is an outstanding (*layman, clergyman, denominational executive*) who has served our church (*faithfully, diligently, with distinction*) for a period of (*twenty-five, thirty-five, forty-five*) years. There is no one whose election could more clearly have demonstrated the denomination's concern for (*evangelical zeal, consecrated loyalty, ecclesiastical statesmanship*), and at the same time given such (*rich, abundant, significant*) promise of (*efficient, dynamic, practical*) leadership. Catering neither to the extreme (*right, left*) nor to the extreme (*left, right*), (*Mr., Dr., Rev.*) Blank stands as a (*rallying, focal, mid-*) point around which men of whatever persuasion can gather with enthusiasm. His opening remarks

---

[1] The infinitive must be split. It always is.

to the (*meeting, assembly, conference*) will long live in (*the hearts of those who heard them, the testimony of the church across the ages, the annual report of our denomination*). He was particularly compelling in his prophetic assertion that ours is the ("*bridge*," "*bridge*," "*bridge*") church, with which others must join to achieve a united Christendom, thereby demonstrating the depth and range of his ecumenical approach.

Impressive, too, was the Report of the (*Social Action, Interchurch Relations, Pensions*) Committee. The chairman of the committee made a number of (*thought-provoking, convention-defying, forward-looking*) suggestions, and in each case the (*assembly, meeting, conference*) voted overwhelmingly to (*give the matter further study for a period of two years, return the report to the committee for clarification, recommend implementation at the local level as soon as the details had been worked out in the national office*).

The most significant aspect of the meetings was the way in which the delegates realized the importance of (*implementing, gearing in, carrying out*) our decisions at the grass roots of our denominational life.[2] This means that the responsibility is placed (*squarely, directly, unavoidably*) upon the local church.

I therefore recommend, Mr. Chairman, that we (*appoint a committee, appoint a subcommittee, ask the pastor*) to prayerfully consider the material from the (*assembly, meeting, conference*) and at some time in the future, when (*they have, he has*) had a chance to study it, give us an

---

[2] It occurs to me in this connection that we need a new denominational verb, the verb "to grassroot." This would avoid all sorts of clumsy constructions such as "to-make-relevant-to-all-areas-of-our-constituency" or "to-implement-at-every-level-down-to-the-local-church-and-up-again." How much simpler to say, "Let's grassroot this!" or even, "This ought to be grassrooted."

evaluation of it, and point out ways in which we could prayerfully consider implementing [3] these proposals. Let us not be found napping in these (*crucial hours, dark days, momentous times*)!

THE EASY WAY

I AM INDEBTED to the advertising strategies of an ortho-dox evangelist for a way of getting my heretical work done with greater dispatch. (What heretic ever lived who was not eager to beat the orthodox on their own playing field?) The idea is disarmingly simple: make Christianity as easy as possible. It is not hard, for example, to make a "decision for Christ" even if you have been sitting in a high balcony, if you can make your way to the foot of the cross (as you can) via escalator. And you needn't worry about being uncomfortable while you're listening to the sermon because, as the advertisements remind you, the place is air-conditioned.

Now, my proposal is also simple: merely adapt this kind of approach to the local church. If enough attention is put on the ease and comfort of the surroundings, people will miss the demands and sternness of the gospel.

In all candor, I must admit that the application on the local church level, the grassrooting, is not solely mine. Somebody has already beaten me to the draw, for I know of churches that advertise that if you arrive too late to get a seat in the nave, there are "comfortable overflow

---

[3] Here, obviously, is the place to say, "grassrooting."

chapels" to accommodate you. This is, I suppose, appropriate to a comfortably accommodating gospel, and suggests that a well-known hymn may need revision:

> He leadeth me: O blessed thought!
> To air-conditioned chapels fraught
> With cushioned pews — where I may see
> The minister on closed TV.

Verily, those who go there will have their own reward. But The Easy Way can be exploited by other means as well.

For example, appeals could be launched to "Join the Episcopal High School Youth Group (Only Church in Town That Lets You Dance)." Or a doorbell-ringing campaign could be instituted on the pitch: "Look here, my man, you've got just the build for our Lutheran Men's Club. We've got the best bowling team in the local church league." Or a quiet, confidential phone call could go: "My *dear*, you simply *must* join the Congregational Women's Circle. We have the most *divine* time sewing. That's *all* we do. You don't need to worry that you'll get caught in one of those em*barr*assing situations where you'll have to *pray* in *public*. And as for keeping up on what's going on in town . . ." Or, finally, a mailing campaign could be initiated with the slogan, "The Methodist Church needs you — you need The Methodist Church," which being translated is: "Man to man, now, here's the story. Don't worry that we're going to make you do a lot of work. We simply need to get our church roll up to two thousand members before the annual report is sent in. And remember, your weekly offerings are deductible from your income tax."

How infinitely superior all this is to letting the notion get abroad that if you joined the Youth Group, some demands might be put upon you! How much safer for the men to bowl than to talk about the relationship of the faith to their businesses! How fortunate for the members of the sewing circle that they run no risk of bumping up against the third chapter of James and its comments about the gossiping tongue! How splendid that the church that is out for new members on any terms never need pause to hear the words, "Because you are lukewarm, and neither cold nor hot, I will spew you out of my mouth."

It looks, in fact, as though we'd better rewrite one more hymn:

> Jerusalem the golden,
>   With milk and honey blest!
> Our local church is better,
>   'Tis not with heat oppressed;
> Our minister is kindly,
>   He never gives offense,
> Our congregation blindly
>   Pays off its debt immense.

GETTING INTO THE STAMP ACT

A church in Florida is now giving Green Stamps
for church attendance.
                                            — news item.

HERE, if anywhere, is proof that piety pays. Not only can you reap spiritual benefits by attending public worship, but if you do so often enough, you can reap further benefits as well — a plated cocktail shaker, a rotisserie, or if you are particularly faithful, an Evinrude outboard motor. Augustine's eschatological hope has been realized: the City of God and the city of man are one.

The idea is bound to spread. Soon newcomers to a town will choose a church that gives the same brand of stamps as the supermarket. Cryptic references such as "S & H" will appear on the outdoor bulletin boards, communicating the fact that it really pays off to go to this church, in this world as well as the next. The uninitiated will probably think that S & H stands for "Salvation & Heaven," the traditional reward offered by churches in the past. But the spiritually sophisticated will know that Salvation and Heaven have been demythologized. Instead of being future hopes, they are present possibilities, for salvation into a stainless-steel and chrome heaven is now possible by turning the stamps in for free gifts. That the gifts are secured at Redemption Centers (*sic*, so help me) indicates the degree to which a new mythology has already been established.

It would be intriguing to learn the terms on which the church in Florida awards its stamps for attendance. The rule in the supermarkets is clear: one stamp for every ten cents' worth of merchandise. But what is the "w-e" (worship-equivalent) of ten cents' worth of merchandise? Ten minutes of worship? Five minutes of *sincere* worship? Or should stamps be given in proportion to the size of the individual's weekly offering? If so, a $5.00-a-week Christian might get fifty stamps, a 50-cent cheapskate five. Since the stamps cost the merchandiser only $\frac{1}{4}$ of a cent each, any merchandiser would be ahead, even with the nickel-nursers.[1]

As an adaptation of the supermarket device of giving double stamp value on days when sales volume tends to slump, extra stamps could be offered for attendance at Sunday-evening services. On these terms, it might even be possible to reclaim the midweek prayer meeting. Works of supererogation could be encouraged, so that by going to both "identical morning services" one could accumulate extra stamps for his friends. Indeed, a sort of surplus stamp fund could be established (a Treasury of Stamps, we might call it), on which individuals could draw when their own resources were depleted and their present salvation depended upon the immediate acquisition of an electric coffeepot or a pair of brass andirons.

> When the stamps in the booklets mount,
> The wife her gifts begins to count.
>   (Tetzel, revised.)

But there are broader and deeper issues than these. For competition is the very life of the trade-stamp world, and

---

[1] Sensitive readers may substitute for the word "merchandiser" the words "session" or "vestry."

competition would inevitably carry over into the ecclesiastical stamp mart as well. Which stamps, then, for whom?

Green Stamps may be all right for Episcopalians, since they look like Greenbacks, of which Episcopalians reputedly have more per capita than lesser breeds without the law. Anglicans, however, who do not like the proletarian association with Greenbacks may prefer that their denomination dispense the more bourgeois-sounding Blue Chip Stamps. But Green Stamps are, according to their promoters, worth 17 percent more than other leading brands, which must be just about the degree of extra worth that a doctrine of assured apostolic succession confers upon the Salvation & Heaven hopes of those who enjoy the blessings of the True Episcopate.

Presbyterians, however, surely cannot give Green Stamps. It is obvious that they will have to offer Plaid Stamps as a means of emphasizing their distinctively Scottish heritage. To be sure, a Scot, particularly a Scots Presbyterian, is not a man to wince at a principle or two for the sake of a 17 percent better return on his investment. But if the price be bishops, as in this case it is, we can be sure that wince he will. We must therefore give Presbyterians a corner on Plaid Stamps, provided they are not too exclusive in dispensing them.

Perhaps, to relieve the situation, a leading Presbyterian statesman could propose terms on which other denominations might unite for the purpose of receiving the fullest possible stamp benefits. Such a proposal might be called The Bleak Proposal.

Methodists and ecumenically minded Baptists, both of whom boast large memberships and are likewise skilled in the art of promotion, should lay claim to Top Value Stamps — a term that accords with the sectarian spirit of adventure, freedom, voluntary association, and the many other qualities connected with frontier ruggedness and the American Way of Life. Nonecumenically minded Baptists will certainly want to preempt Triple S Blue Stamps (submission, submersion, and secession in that order). Sects-in-the-process-of-becoming-churches, and trying to be very up-to-date about it, will probably want their stamps in gorgeous technicolor. If so, they can offer combination values from among the following brands: National Red Stamps, Gift House Blue Stamps, Orange Stamps, Orange Thrifty Stamps, Gold Bond Stamps, and Gold Strike Stamps. Color-blind sectarians can settle for Eagle Stamps, although even these give off a subtle aura of red, white, and blue. We can let Congregationalists who have not yet joined the United Church have Community Stamps, and still have Mor Valu Stamps and King Korn Stamps left over for any groups as yet uncommitted.

In time, of course, stamps will replace money in the American economy, and provide a new and convenient form of currency. In fact, the way things are going, it won't be long before the supermarkets are simply selling stamps, and giving away free food as an inducement to stamp buyers. What this may mean for the churches I must leave to my readers to determine.

FOIBLES FOR OUR TIMES

(With Apologies to That Gentle Heretic James Thurber)

ONE of my correspondents has asked for a column "for the Young People." It is her feeling that Improving Tales can be of use in Keeping Young People Out Of Trouble. Particularly in these days of the decline of the story sermon, I have felt it important to work out a few tales that can be told to the young for their edification and enlightenment and advancement in moral rectitude.

THE MAN AND HIS THREE FINE DAUGHTERS

Once upon a time there was a father who had always been on the straight and narrow. Never once had he been tempted to go off the wagon, because at the age of eleven he took the pledge.

One summer, however, he went on a pleasure cruise with his wife and their three fine daughters.

The spirit of adventure prevailed upon the three fine daughters, and they sought their father's permission to enter the ship's bar and have a drink, "just this once," as they put it, for although they too had taken the pledge, they were, after all, Modern Youth.

After hearing their many and importunate pleadings, the father finally said: "Very well. You may have a drink," he went on, "of the nasty stuff," he continued, "so that you will nevermore," he emphasized, "crave it. But," he added, "we will all go in together." (For he had heard tales of what sometimes happens to young ladies, even in groups of three, who go unescorted into ships' bars.)

So the father and his wife and their three fine daughters entered the bar, and the father boldly ordered sherry (straight) all around.

While they were sipping their sherry, a tanker rammed the luxury liner amidships and they perished one and all.

MORAL: *The family that drinks together sinks together.*

THE MAN IN THE GRAY FLANNEL GOOF

Once upon a time there was a man who had unadvisedly gotten himself involved with two women. He continually showered presents upon them, being careful always to give blue presents to the one and pale-green presents to the other. For each woman was jealous of her hold upon the man, and had the woman who desired blue presents received pale-green ones, or the woman who desired pale-green presents received blue ones, each would have realized that something was askew.

So the man was very careful.

But one time the man, having just made a killing on the stock market, became confused, for success had gone to his head.

And sure enough! He gave the woman who was expecting blue presents a pale-green brooch, and he gave the woman who was expecting pale-green presents a blue dress. And to each of them in turn, so flustered had he become, he made the same speech: "Darling, I have brought you a gift in your favorite color." And from each of them in return he received identical treatment, a shiner that was approximately the color of blue and pale green combined.

He never recovered his touch on the Stock Market, and was soon the laughing stock of the business world.

MORAL: *No man can serve two mistresses.*

THE PREACHER MAN AND THE HEATHEN NATION

Once upon a time there was a preacher man who wanted to convert a heathen nation. So he got himself a pulpit, and he got himself a copy of the Good Book, and he trained his lungs for six months by shouting above the roar of Niagara Falls, and then he took himself off to the heathen nation.

He set up his pulpit in the main square of the largest city, during a peace demonstration, and he got out his copy of the Good Book, and he spoke a word in season to the assembled multitudes. And so great was the power of his lungs that even the pilots in the jet planes overhead overheard and were astonished.

But pretty soon the Secret Police took the preacher man off to headquarters and roughed him up a bit. Then they told him that he could not speak in their country, and that anyway he had no more chance of converting the people assembled in the square than he had of converting Niagara Falls itself. The preacher man pointed out that they had their own brand of preacher man speaking through the loudspeakers all over the square and throughout the land.

But they only scoffed at him and pushed him over the nearest boundary.

MORAL: *Truth has not the same rights as error.*

EXPANDING THE CHURCH YEAR

A FEW of the 365 days of the year have not yet been given official ecclesiastical designation. This is a grievous oversight which I propose to remedy. We need more feast days, holy days, and saints days so that the liturgical concerns of contemporary Christians can be given their due.

World Series time, for example, would be a convenient time to appropriate the pagan rites of the ball field, simply by recognizing them for what they are — the most profoundly religious gestures in the whole of American culture. This part of the church year could therefore be officially designated as *The Feast of St. Hank and St. Mickey (Hankmickmas Day)*, or even unofficially as *The Veneration of Aaron's Mantle*.

The feast is celebrated in the afternoon, at a long service lasting from about two to five P.M., although evening services have received increasing liturgical sanction. Worship takes place in a large and airy sanctuary specially designed for the occasion, in which the worshipers sit in pews surrounding the priests and high priests. The archaic custom of pew rents is still observed, and there seems little likelihood that it will be replaced by voluntary offerings.

Those who actually conduct the service are the priests and high priests. The *priests* wear vestments of white or light gray, a hat being required of each priest if his actions are to be counted as valid ones. The priests are further distinguishable by their employment of ecclesiastical language: references to Deity are frequently uttered during the spiritual exercises.

The *high priests* have ultimate authority over the activities of the priests. They can say to any one of the priests, "Go!" and he goeth, right out of the sanctuary. They are garbed in a way more traditionally associated with ecclesiastical life, wearing black vestments. Their ecclesiastical vocabulary is limited to a few monosyllabic utterances ("Strike!" "Ball!" "Out!" "Safe!" etc.), but these are coupled with certain cultic gestures (such as the hands outspread, palms down, or the up-jerked thumb) that render their meaning plain to all the worshipers.

The lay worshipers come appropriately clad for the cultic rites, usually minus coat and tie. They do not actually participate in the worship itself, although they share vicariously in all that the priests do. Laymen must be particularly careful not to overstep their appointed bounds. Should a lay worshiper, for example, venture into the green-carpeted portion of the sanctuary, he will be removed from the premises by a verger, or, if necessary, a group of vergers, each appropriately clad in black and wearing the ancient symbol of authority, the holster.

Certain cultic rites are reserved for laymen, however, which add immeasurably to the "meaningfulness" of the service. For one thing, they experience a real sense of *koinōnia* with other leather-lunged Americans, participating in chants and antiphonal responses reserved for the lay worshipers ("Kill the umpire!" "We want a hit!" etc.) and eating and drinking together. A special point is made at all services, in fact, of offering the worshipers frequent opportunity to partake of the good gifts of creation, especially those derived from malt and hops. There is a directly observable ratio between the frequency of libation and the increase in communal participation.

The most important cultic practice, however, is the one of exercising the traditional lay prerogative of *the right of private judgment.* This involves active disagreement with the ruling of one or more of the high priests. Since the laymen are convinced that they occupy vantage points of observation far superior to those of the high priests themselves, it is only natural that they should attempt to correct the bizarre decisions that the high priests make. To be sure, the decisions of the high priests are "irreformable," even if they are not necessarily "infallible," but no layman will admit this. He indicates allegiance to the doctrine of the high priesthood of all believers, and acknowledgment of a priestly hierarchy is vociferously disavowed, even though the high priests always have the last word.

The worshiper does not leave his religion in the sanctuary. He leaves, on the contrary, motivated by high ethical concern, recognizing the importance of implementing his faith. He says, with a look of dedication in his eyes, and an unspoken assertion of *credo quia absurdum est* in his heart, "Next time we'll murder the bums."

THREE EASY WAYS TO SPOIL CHRISTMAS, OR "HARK! THE HERALD SQUARE ANGELS SING"

CHRISTMASTIME often leads to a resurgence of faith. But it need not. Those things which are most dangerous to heresy also afford heresy its greatest opportunity. I, for one, am willing to take the chance that a few people will act selflessly in a spirit of riotous charity, in exchange for the opportunity that Christmas provides of undermining the faith of basically well-intentioned people.

The rule for advancing heresy during the Christmas season is a very simple one. It is: Go Them One Better. All the Christmas customs can serve our purposes, but three are particularly valuable.

1. Take this matter of Christmas carols. They positively exude orthodoxy. ("Veiled in flesh the Godhead see; Hail th'Incarnate Deity.") If people ever thought seriously about the words, the whole world would be turned upside down. But the faulty conclusion should not be drawn that carols are to be discouraged. No. The thing to do is to *promote* them. Have them sung all the time, not only in the church and at church gatherings, but at Rotary, P.T.A., the Lions, the Elks, the regional conferences of all the corporations, the biennial gatherings at Atlantic City. Petition department stores to play recordings of carols all through the working day to foster "the Christmas spirit." Suggest that the Chamber of

Commerce install a P.A. system to play carols on the town common during the noon hour. Write to the producers of the innumerable shows on television, pleading that stars of stage and screen be drafted to sing carols over the ether waves.

All this activity will pay dividends, for it will lead to one of two reactions: (1) Some people will become so bored with the constant repetition that they won't pay any more attention to the subject matter of the carols than they pay to TV commercials they have seen twenty times over. (The comparison, after all, is apt. What is a carol but a kind of commercial for God?) (2) And the other people will become so furious with the constant repetition that they will come to entertain a positive dislike, if not hatred, for Christmas and all that goes along with it.

2. Another way to spoil Christmas is to promote to the point of nausea the normal and healthy instinct to give. (We can always count on tremendous help here from all the advertising concerns.) There is, after all, something incongruous about buying a miniature Christmas sleigh full of Invisible Veil Face Powder and jumbo lipstick. There is something grotesque (not to say theologically inconsistent) about buying an angel doll with a removable halo. And it is surely a poor symbol of the everlasting and indestructible nature of our Christmas wishes to convey these via "a Christmas card you can eat," made of a certain well-known brand of chocolate. One manufacturer goes so far as to offer "cherubs in tall spirits," a set of highball glasses, each with a Christmas angel who is "captioned," so that presumably you get the same one on the second round. (Imagine the gastronomical upsets resulting from mixing your angels, and taking a Michael and a Gabriel in quick succession!)

3. A third chance to exploit Christmas for the cause of heresy is in the embarrassingly fertile field of Christmas cards, whether edible or not. The pitch, it seems to me, should be to send cards as far removed from the theme of Christmas as possible, and the manufacturers have provided us with these in abundance. Item: a card in stunning modern design and color, which contains nothing at all but a cigarette resting on an ash tray, its smoke curling up in the air to form the words "Merry Xmas" (*sic*). The Pickwickian motif is a good evasion too — a card on which the color green usually predominates, featuring a number of bulbous-nosed gentlemen in green tights standing around a fireplace, smoking long-stemmed pipes and quaffing tankards of ale. A hearty scene, to be sure, calculated to relate Christmas to "That Sort of Thing," and carefully calculated to remind no one of a manger or a cross.

Indeed, the possibilities for the exploitation of heresy at Christmastime are endless. And I would call upon all my followers to take seriously this annual opportunity which is handed them, so that we may gather together after the day itself and encourage one another with our own private carol:

> Now let us be merry,
>   Drive sorrow away,
> For heresy's children
>   Are spawned on this day.

PART TWO

The World's Important Religions

(A SERIES)

❧

I. AMERICANITY — 2. NATURISM — 3. LINGOISM —
4. CHURCHIANITY

A FEW YEARS ago *Life* magazine ran a series to give its readers an education in "The World's Great Religions." I was struck not only by the wealth of information which this series placed at the disposal of *Life*'s viewers, but also by the fact that so many of the world's *important* religions were omitted. By "important" I mean the religions to which people really give themselves, the religions to which men turn in the great crises of life, i.e., when the chips are down or when things are going exceptionally well. And although I will have to do it without pictures, I nevertheless make bold to offer a series of descriptions of four of the world's important religions.

---

1. AMERICANITY

ALTHOUGH this is a religion of fairly recent origin as world religions go (it is less than two hundred years old as I count time), it has in recent years become, so its adherents would claim, the most important. It cannot with total accuracy be called a *world* religion, since there are still a great many people in such colonies as Europe, Asia, Africa, the Far East, the Near East, and the Arctic and Antarctic regions who have not yet been converted by its missionaries, though in the last-named region there have been some indications recently of a shift of sentiment among the Penguins.

Even in the Patristic Period, e.g., of the early church fathers, or as they are called in this case, the "founding fathers," there were hints as to the direction in which the final *creedal formulations* of this religion would crystallize. But it was a sentiment from the high Middle Ages that, clearly capturing the sense of total commitment demanded by any true religion, best epitomized the faith of the true adherents. This sentiment went (and still goes), "My country, right or wrong; may she always be right, but right or wrong, my country." This absolute devotion to the claims of the deity has become more rather than less important in the later development of the religion.

Another creed of Americanity, which its apostles preach by their actions, and which is hence called the "apostles' creed," begins something like this: "I believe in America the nation almighty, creator of heaven on earth." Variant readings make it impossible to quote the creed in its entirety, but it is significant that in no surviving rescension is there any reference to crucifixion, death, or burial. This is one religion that has a rising, but never a dying, savior-god.

Americanity has its own *eschatology*, or doctrine of the last things. When an adherent of the faith is asked about the meaning of history, where history is going, and in what he places his ultimate trust and hope, the answer is given by the phrase, "the American century." (Strange irony, indeed, that *Life* failed to give explicit attention to this religion. Sometimes, apparently, it is the better part of journalistic wisdom not to let the left hand know what the right hand is doing.) Coupled with this eschatology is a highly developed *doctrine of the church*, or *the means of salvation*. This doctrine is expressed in the classic words *extra Americam nulla salus* (outside America there is no salvation). The meaning of this doctrine is quite clear to adherents of the faith, and they hold it as a literal truth. No poor benighted European Continentals, or British socialists, or Indian neutralists, have a chance of entering the Kingdom of Man until they have been completely converted to Americanity. And those so-called Americans who want to participate in interfaith conferences with other nations, carrying on united negotiations (sometimes called "u.n." for short) are clearly dangerous.

How is this faith passed on from generation to generation? This is done in highly orthodox fashion by a doctrine of *apostolic succession*, in which purity of belief, however, is guaranteed not by a laying on of hands but by transmission through the right wing. This perhaps accounts for the fact that nonbelievers sometimes refer to the stance of this faith as "ostrichlike," a phrase that evokes peculiar horror on the part of the faithful, and prompts them to reply that their attackers are so angry that they are "seeing red."

The *doctrines* of the faith are many and varied, but they have usually grown up out of a specific *Sitz im Leben*. Thus, for example, at one time in the history of the faith there was a doctrine known as the Monroe Doctrine. Recently, this has been modified by renaming it the Marilyn Monroe Doctrine, after a now deceased goddess, and involves sending photographs of the one from whom the doctrine derives its name to every portion of the mission field, where the apostles of Americanity are stationed in their ecclesiastical barracks. This has the two-fold advantage of reminding the apostles what it is they are defending (every one of them being a *defensor fidei*), and also of pointing out to the adherents of other faiths the superior advantages of the culture produced by the religion of Americanity.

Wherein lies the great appeal of this religion? Most significantly perhaps in (1) the assurance with which it can claim to be the final hope of mankind; (2) the exclusiveness with which it can assert in the name of its deity, "Thou shalt have no other gods before me," which in a briefer and more up-to-date translation goes, "America First"; (3) the wisdom of its benevolence program and almsgiving, which demands only that the recipients subscribe 100 percent to the creed of Americanity; and (4) the dedication of its priest-group, all of whom are prepared that heaven and earth should quite literally pass away before one jot or tittle of their creed be modified.

2. NATURISM

I N CONTRAST to Americanity, which persists in season and out of season, Naturism is a seasonal cult whose popularity waxes and wanes with the temperature and the time of year. It is not, for example, the most popular religious faith in the middle of a March blizzard, nor does it usually gather its full quota of adherents when the temperature is hovering around 107 degrees in the shade.

But in the summertime, in places where there are cool breezes, mountain vistas, forest glades, sylvan lakes (how easily the phrases from the devotional literature of the faith come to mind!), the adherents of Naturism begin to go on a spiritual spree once more, and a delightful kind of heresy once again reasserts itself. To be sure, with the coming of winter, the popularity of the cult dies down. But a couple of months of heresy each summer are quite enough to innoculate the believer against the real thing for the intervening ten months.

The gods of Naturism usually receive fullest homage at the interfaith gatherings known as Summer Conferences. At such places there is *usually* a Cathedral of the Pines, in which worshipers are directed to meditate upon the beauty and straightness of the trees rather than upon the Creator of the trees. At such places there is *always* an Inspiration Point. It may look out upon a lake shore, it may look out upon a mountain — but whatever it looks out on, it will be just loaded with Inspiration. To be sure, the *content* of the Inspiration is very hard to define, but all Inspiration Points have at least this much in common religiously: they are soothing rather than demanding. Indeed, I am thinking of offering an annual St. Hereticus Medal to the first summer conference each year to report that it has no Inspiration Point, with second place going to the one honest enough to admit that *its* Inspiration Point is heavily infested with mosquitoes or black flies.

Do not overlook the reference to the "*gods* of Naturism" at the beginning of the last paragraph. For if one asks about the deity worshiped by the Naturists, the reply always has to be given in the plural, for this is polytheism with a vengeance. The devotees of Naturism, however, practice a high degree of selectivity in the choice of gods who may inhabit their pantheon. They acknowledge the god of the sunset (peaceful and calming), the god of the starry night ("inspirational"), the god of the sky-blue lake waters (comforting), and the god of the storm-seen-at-a-distance (majestic and awe-inspiring). But they over-look or deliberately fail to worship the god of the forest fire (wantonly destructive), the god of the jungle animals (wantonly destructive), the god of the poisonous mush-room (wantonly destructive), and the god of the lightning bolt that killed a three-year-old child (wantonly de-structive).

There are numerous cultic sayings and ritualistic prac-tices by means of which the believers in Naturism can be distinguished. There is, for example, the familiar phrase, "Finding God through nature," with its interesting im-plication that God has gotten lost. There is the phrase, "Through Nature to Nature's God," a highly original inversion of the attitude found in the Bible. And there is the rubric, "Kneel when you light a fire," with its implication that you are thereby engaging in an act of reverence. Perhaps so. But in the rather more sordid circles in which I am sometimes forced to travel, I have discovered that the act of kneeling is likewise associated with the incantation, "Seven come eleven" or the manna-producing versicle, "Roll them bones!" These may likewise bespeak acts of reverence, but surely they are to a different deity.

Thus we find among the varieties of Naturism such well-defined subcults as *woodsology*, featuring forest glades or sylvan beauty; *sunsetism*, featuring canoe prows or pine trees in the foreground and flaming colors in the background; and *campfirology*, in which worshipers sit crosslegged in a circle (symbol of eternity) and gaze into the fire (symbol of transitoriness) and sing "*Vive la compagnie*" (symbol of fellowship). *Campfirology*, however, must not be confused with *camphorology*, a ritualistic practice engaged in during the month of June, designed to keep winter vestments safe during the summer months from that ingenious little creation of the god of nature, the moth.

The most popular form of Naturanity, however, is the *Tee cult*. The creed of this cult is very brief, indicating that the cult is still young, for no anathemas have yet been added at the end of it. The creed goes, "I believe (*Credo*) that you can worship God better on the golf course than you can in church." (Such are the linguistic peculiarities of this creed that for "you" one must read "I" throughout.)

Members of the cult demonstrate their devotion to the creed by making their Stations of the Course (18 in number) each Sunday morning. Along with this goes a type of sacramental experience known as *tee-drinking*, by means of which an extraordinary sense of good fellowship is stimulated, sometimes to the extent that the believers break forth in songs of praise — or what must be *assumed* to be songs of praise, since the words are not always readily distinguishable.

In sum, all the varieties of Naturism are such as to fill the heart of the heretic with joy, precisely because Naturism is *so close* to the real thing that it can often be mistaken for it. All it really does that is wrong is to take the things God has created and make those things into gods. Making things into gods . . .

I, Hereticus, and I write it with my own hand, could ask for no more. And I need not worry that the believers in Naturism will read my words and see the folly of their ways. No. They will be too busy watching the sunset.

3. LINGOISM

PERHAPS the most popular world religion of all is Lingoism. The Lingoist is bewitched by the power of words; he believes that by saying certain words and phrases often enough he will be able to produce the effect of belief. His favorite Scriptural text (ripped violently out of context and given a meaning not intended by its author) is, "In the beginning was the *word*." If he believes in conversion, it is conversion by cliché; if he believes in salvation, it is salvation by semantics. In his faith, crosses are replaced by creeds. Rather than invocation to God, he has intonation about God. Instead of parading pious practices, he practices pious platitudes.

Now there are all sorts and conditions of this breed. Some of the most effective Lingoists are the young men just out of seminaries. They have picked up an astonishing vocabulary, useful no doubt in discussions with their peers, which they inflict upon unsuspecting congregations for months or even years, until they discover that although Yahweh may have created the heavens by the word of his mouth (Ps. 33:6), they are not going to save the heathen by the words of their mouths.

There are several ways of spotting a recently converted Lingoist in the pulpit:

a. He probably uses the word "encounter" a good deal. A perfectly good word, "encounter," describing a perfectly real experience. But somehow it gets spoiled when it is just talked about. It is one thing to preach *about* encounter every Sunday, but it is quite another thing to bring people to the place where, through the sermon, they actually *do* encounter the living God. Fortunately for my own vested interests, the former situation almost universally prevails in the Protestant pulpit today.

b. Another favorite word is "mansexistentialsituation," which is usually described by contrasting "thebiblicalview" (translated "profound") with "thegreekmind" (translated "shallow"). Now it might or might not be the case that thebiblicalview and thegreekmind are, respectively, profound and shallow; but to establish this fact more is needed than a few handy quotes from a seminary professor, which is the sort of evidence that the Lingoist usually produces. Here, too, as at most other points, the Lingoist is proceeding on the basis of a faith gotten second-hand.

c. Another phrase in the Lingoist's vocabulary goes, "Our-moral-progress-has-not-kept-up-with-our-technical-achievements." If this is said enough times in the course of a speech or a sermon, the Lingoist can usually persuade somebody besides himself that it is true, though who would ever have doubted it in the first place is something else again.

But it is not simply the poor parson who is the Lingoist. He will probably win many converts among his laymen, who will produce their own creedal formulations. One bit of lay lingo directed again and again at the poor parson is the reiterated demand, "Give me a simple answer." And it is very hard to tell the layman that perhaps the answers to profound questions have to be profound, and that simple answers can only be given to simple (i.e., inconsequential) questions. An expanded version of the "Give me a simple answer" formula is the one that goes, "I don't care two cents for theology; all I want is plain, practical, down-to-earth Christianity," which in *its* turn is merely a new variation on the old theme, "It's deeds we need, not creeds." But what happens is that

> To heed
> The need
> For the doing of deeds
> Becomes
> The seed
> For the growth of creeds.

Which means, in cold prose, that if we have a creed about the need for deeds, then we don't have to worry so much about the deeds themselves.

The lay Lingoist usually has a belief in salvation by statistics as well: "One hundred new members before Easter." Or: "Is he a good minister? You bet. Worth sixty-seven hundred and parsonage any day. Keeps the church on an even keel." Or, "Upped the church budget $3,200 this year." (This latter bit of lingo is not to be confused with the *means* of upping the budget. This is known as bingo.)

The conservatives have their lingo too. The words become so familiar to their hearers by constant repetition that it doesn't matter where you divide them. We recognize immediately, "Doyou believeinthe substitutionary-doctrineof theatonement?" or, "Prep areto meetthyGod." One sometimes feels that their most reiterated question could be given new effectiveness if it were streamlined after the manner of modern advertising techniques so that it read, "R U saved?"

The most significant and revealing symbol of the Lingo-ist position is the phrase, "The Judeo-Christian tradition." For this is a convenient way of avoiding statements that begin with those clumsy words, "*I* believe . . ." To say that "the Judeo-Christian tradition affirms" need involve no personal commitment at all. How much pleasanter, indeed, to say, "It emerges as a clear consensus in the development of the prophetic strain of the Judeo-Christian tradition that the conception of God is one which involves both the notions of justice and mercy," than to have to say, point-blank, "I believe that God both condemns and forgives me."

This illustrates, from the heretic's point of view, the real beauty of Lingoism. It means — and this has been a consistent strain in all of the above illustrations — that people can always have their faith at second hand. It means that they can satisfy "their religious impulses" by talking *about* something, rather than (frightening thought) having to experience Someone. It means that they are always trying, and always succeeding, in keeping God at arm's length.

And that is just what we want.

4. CHURCHIANITY

FOR years I have been plugging a maxim which goes, "I believe in Christianity but not in Churchianity." This old saw has had a useful life, but its teeth are now dulled from overuse. And rather than try to sharpen it up again, I suggest a new heretical maxim for the twentieth century, which is simply an inversion of the old one. The new one could not be spoken aloud, so manifestly absurd would it sound, but it could be subtly introduced into current discussion in such a way as to enable heresy to flourish anew with all the vigor of the green bay tree. It would go, of course, "I believe in Churchianity" — with the unspoken assumption tacked on at the end — ". . . but not in Christianity." Some such idea is an absolute necessity in this day and age when the ecumaniacs are getting dangerously close to suggesting that the body of Christ can once again be clothed in a seamless robe.

Churchianity implies salvation by denominational exclusiveness. It should no longer be enough for the believer to confess his faith in Jesus Christ as his Lord and Savior. Such an allegiance should be refined by reference to a more ultimate fidelity — faith in the particular branch of Christendom to which the believer belongs.

The easiest way to promote Churchianity, of course, is to run down other denominations. We have known for centuries that heretical polemics flourish best in a negative atmosphere. Witness how successful we have been in making Protestants define their faith in negative terms — "protesters" *against* certain aspects of Roman Catholicism, for example. That this misses the whole point of the Reformation is a fact for which I remain profoundly grateful, and I say (in all humility, of course) that much of its widespread acceptance is due to my influence.

Thus the simplest procedure for the adherent of Churchianity is to use emotionally charged words which by means of their inflection indicate disapproval. Here are a few such words, punctuated to indicate the type of inflection desired: "spike!" "*Meth*odist!" "nonepiscopal . . ." "*lit*urgy?" (followed by the incredulous under-the-breath comment, ". . . in *our* church?") "tradition-bound . . ." "*pap*ish!" Another way to achieve the same effect is to suggest that while *other* denominations may go back to some humanly instituted point of origin ("Rome," "Canterbury," "Geneva," "Wittenberg"), *our* denomination goes back to the real point of origin ("the apostolic community," say, or "the New Testament church").

But all need not be negative. There are positive ways of thinking that can introduce schism in our own day. I suggest (as is my wont) three principles:

1. *The only true church exists where there are bishops.* Here it need not matter a whit whether the bishops and their flocks exhibit the fruits of the Spirit, just so long as there are bishops. The fruits of the Spirit can take care of themselves. They are a kind of bonus, whose existence is pleasant and to be hoped for, but they are not at all essential (of the *bene esse*, perhaps, but not of the *esse* of the church). All sorts of new alignments and fresh divi-

sions could result from taking this position seriously. Imagine how confusing it would have been to have heard Bromley Oxnam and Francis Spellman arguing on the same side of an issue!

2. *The only true church exists where there is a democratic form of government.* This has the advantage of appealing to the layman, and being very modern and up-to-date. Surely any authoritarian or autocratic form of church government is out of keeping with the twentieth century. Churches that are "bishop ridden" or "controlled from above" are clearly totalitarian. "A democratic church for a democratic nation" — the slogan would look well on subway posters. It could even be printed on small cards for mass distribution in balloons and sent behind the Iron Curtain. And if a theological base be desired for this position, it can surely be suggested that the very doctrine of the Trinity implies that God is a sort of democracy himself.

3. *The only true church is the "bridge" church.* This is a splendid one. It is splendid because every denomination in existence has demonstrated conclusively, to itself, that *it* is the real bridge church, containing the true fullness of the faith, and gathering up in itself the partial and incomplete witness of every other denomination. Furthermore, the size of the denomination making the claim need be of no account here, since appeal can always be made to that most excellent maxim of St. Arius, "Great yolks from little Leghorns grow."

PART THREE

Making the Bible Relevant: Biblical Needs and How to Meet Them

❧

THE NEED FOR A NEW TRANSLATION — THE NEED FOR SOME
NEW EDITIONS — THE NEED FOR SOME NEW ADDITIONS – I
— THE NEED FOR SOME NEW ADDITIONS – II

THE NEED FOR A NEW TRANSLATION

H ow can we interest *intelligent* people in the faith?"
more than one church executive has asked on
more than one occasion.

Well, I've found a way. What we need is a new translation of the Bible. The form this translation should take
came to me as I was scanning some old best-seller lists
and noted that a consistent winner for many weeks had
been *Winnie Ille Pu*. This translation of an old English
classic into Latin — a daring reversal of the more familiar
formula of translating an old Latin classic into English —
has apparently had numerous benefits for all concerned.
For one thing, it is now a mark of social sophistication to
have *Winnie Ille Pu* sitting on one's coffee table. Further-

more, people have started reading the old English version again, apparently needing a "trot" when the going gets hard. The sale of Latin-English dictionaries has undoubtedly been aided, thus putting hard money into circulation once more. And people otherwise separated by linguistic boundaries have now found a common bond; yea more, a common tongue.

Why not, I mused, pondering these facts, learn from our separated brethren in the commercial world, and by a similar device recapture the sophisticated intelligentsia for the faith? The gimmick for achieving this came to me in a flash — a moment of inspiration, I am tempted to call it — daring in its simplicity and yet also daring in its implications: *a Latin Bible*.

I know that the conservatives among my readers will immediately object to the practicality, if not the wisdom, of such a venture. But none of the objections, I am convinced, can begin to outweigh the advantages of proceeding immediately to do for Joseph and Amos and Paul what *Winnie Ille Pu* has done for Piglet and Eeyore and Tigger. In simplest terms, if we make it all available in Latin, people will not only leave the translation on their coffee tables, they will also begin to read one of the "trots" still available in English.

Some, of course, will object that since the Bible is considerably longer than *Winnie-the-Pooh*, it would take too long to get the whole thing in good solid Latin. But in these days of ecumenical efficiency, the answer is surely clear: we must get a team of translators, the best scholars of the various denominations, and give each one responsibility for translating a single book. If the committee were to meet about twice a year to check one another's work, we could surely have a smooth Latin translation in, say, five to seven years. It might be called a revised standard version when completed.

Others will object to the cost of such a venture. But if the various denominations were to cooperate on the matter, along with an enterprising publisher, sharing the costs and taking a small investor's gamble (no faith without risk . . .), the losses, even if there were any, could be spread around so as to do no harm to anyone.

The most powerful objection, I feel sure, will come from the Roman Catholic hierarchy. Rome moves slowly, preferring to "wait and see" before rushing aboard the latest doctrinal or promotional fad. And the notion of a Latin translation of the Bible is perhaps *too* daring a one for us to be able to anticipate Roman support — at least for a number of decades. If, however, the venture should prove successful, one could hope for a time when the Roman Catholic Church, while perhaps not approving the sale of the Latin version to its untrained laity, would permit its use by carefully selected seminarians and those who are already members of religious orders.

There are bound to be various other objections, but surely the advantages will outweigh them: (1) If the movement to read the Bible in Latin caught on, we could gradually introduce readings from the new Latin translation into church services, and when people's ears had become accustomed to this, it might in time be possible to render some of the musical portions of the service in the Latin tongue. (2) From there it would be only a step to the use of simple congregational responses in Latin, and even to the introduction of Latin prayers. (3) The compulsory use of Latin in sermons would lead to a revival of expository preaching, since most preachers would know only enough Latin to shift Biblical phrases around and use them as their own. (We must guard against a Latin edition of the *Reader's Digest*, which would furnish them with an overabundance of illustrative material.) (4) Finally, this use of a common tongue (the "vernacular," we might one day call it) could be a means of uniting separated portions of Christendom, since there would no longer be any need to argue about "debts" vs. "trespasses," or whether or not there were any Communists on the RSV translation committee.

THE NEED FOR SOME NEW EDITIONS

A<small>N ENTERPRISING</small> publisher recently issued *The Teen-Age Version of the Holy Bible*. Quite frankly, I expected to find Holy Writ written in a contemporary idiom: "And God leveled with the Israelite kids, saying, 'Get with it, chums!'" All we got, however, was the old King James Version with minimal changes for clarity. Frankly, it's hard to see how the book differs from a whole host of KJV's, save that it has a transparent dust jacket ("keeps the Bible looking like a Bible"), three-color pictures, a glossary of terms (the third of which, curiously enough, is "adulteri"), paragraphing, and a preface.

My purpose, however, is not to pan *The Teen-Age Version of the Holy Bible*. At $7.95 a copy the publishers are going to have a rough enough time as it is. Instead, I pay tribute to it for suggesting a whole new dimension of Bible-publishing, capable of considerably greater daring.

I see, for example, *The Executive's Bible*, so stamped (tastefully, to be sure), shaped like a briefcase, and edited to suit the needs and purposes of its constituency. Certain portions of the text will be deleted, i.e., "You cannot serve God and mammon" (Luke 16:13). Certain other portions will be printed in boldface type. "Make friends for yourselves by means of unrighteous mammon" (Luke 16:9) just happens to come to mind. For an extra $2.95, *The Executive's Bible* will have bound into its gray-flannel lining a copy of Bruce Barton's *The Man Nobody Knows* (recently reissued in paperback), a book that should occupy almost equal canonical status in the life of the Executive.

Special attention can be given to the Executive's Golden Text, "Wist ye not that I must be about my Father's *business?*" (Luke 2:49), a bit of Scripture that made a very, very deep impression upon Mr. Barton. Another verse for boldface treatment would be that one designed for contemplation when one's competitors have stolen a market: "I hate them with perfect hatred; I count them my enemies" (Ps. 139:22). We will, of course, excise reference to the fact that the early Christian community "had all things common; and sold their possessions and goods, and parted them to all men, as every man had need" (Acts 2:44-45). Smacks of Marx. Further reminder: no red covers on *The Executive's Bible*.

Another "must" is *The Sportsman's Bible*, for use on fishing trips and hunting expeditions. A waterproof jacket lined with kapok is called for, complete with built-in compass. The book will contain Biblical maxims dear to the heart of sportsmen (the psalmist's injunction to "Praise the Lord with pipes," for example), a four-color painting of Joseph serving in Pharaoh's court (detachable so that it can be mounted, framed, and hung in the den), an etching of the hart panting after the water brooks, perhaps pursued by a Christian hunter, and a glossary of all the times the word "fish" is mentioned in the Bible. Printed in capital letters or italics could be the Pauline advice, "Use a little wine for the sake of your stomach" (I Tim. 5:23). Protestant and Catholic consultants could be polled in advance about the advisability of including Biblical instances of determining the divine will by a throw of the dice.

Published in time for the next presidential campaign could be a special edition of *The Politician's Bible*. This should be bound in scuffed leather to give the impression of wear and tear incurred by daily use. On the flyleaf could be inscribed, in a simulated feminine scrawl, "To my dear son . . ." The size of the volume ($2\frac{5}{8}'' \times 4\frac{3}{4}''$) should occasion such press dispatches as, "Whipping his well-worn Bible, a gift from his mother, out of his vest pocket, the candidate replied . . ."

References to kings and other national leaders being punished for failing to do the will of God will, of course, be deleted, along with embarrassing passages such as Rev., ch. 13, that compare the state to the beast. This will enable greater prominence to be given to the Biblical insight that a "ruler" (i.e., a politician) is "God's servant for your good."

Politicians advocating a certain type of fiscal policy will want the authority of Holy Writ for their admonition to "Pay . . . taxes to whom taxes are due" (Rom. 13:7). And all politicians, by conflating certain texts with a minimum of dishonesty, will be able to claim direct Scriptural warrant for the stock-in-trade conclusion of every political speech, viz., "This . . . nation . . . under . . . God" (cf. respectively Esther 9:17; Isa. 1:4; Gen. 1:7; II Kings 1:2. New Testament references will be made available for politicians not primarily concerned with "the Jewish vote").

In spite of its limited market at present, work should commence immediately on my newest high-priority project: *The Astronaut's Bible.*

But this requires more space than is available at present.

THE NEED FOR SOME NEW ADDITIONS — I

(A Scripture Lesson for Advent)

SOMEHOW I never made the canon. This is, to any saint, a source of disappointment, particularly when one feels, as I do, that Jude didn't really deserve the honor, either.

But I have recently had my hope renewed, not by my fellow heretics, but by the orthodox. For hath not Barth said, "The canon is not closed"? (Barth, *Die kirchliche Dogmatik*, I/2, para. 19, subsection 2, pp. 473–481, my translation, condensed). I agree. Who am I to challenge Barth? But I can go him one better. I can point out where the canon needs to be extended.

We need a fifth gospel. It could be called (though I may not be the one to initiate the suggestion) The Gospel According to St. Hereticus. I would not claim originality for its message any more than my distinguished colleagues in this company would claim originality for their contributions to the canon. I would claim only that I have been faithful, in a most literal way, to the oral traditions and written records that have been circulating freely in the second half of twentieth-century Christendom.

I shall offer, then, two selections from my gospel, one dealing with Christmas and the other with Easter, as modern Protestantism has come to interpret those events.

Biblical critics should have the same freedom with my gospel that they have with all the others. I will, in fact, help the critics out by identifying some of the sources upon which I have been dependent in composing ch. 2, which shortly follows. These have been the G source (Gimbel's); the various pericopes of the C source (commercials), notably C_r (radio) and C_t (television); the S_2 source (Sunday School); the P source, notably P_1 (pageants) and P_2 (Protestant pulpit); and the C_2 source (Christmas carols). It may be noted by the most discerning that there is occasionally a slight reliance, at considerable remove, on two further multiple sources, the RSV and the KJV, with which, of course, my readers are acquainted.

I have left the text in the American koine, without attempting to rearrange it. This would be to tamper illicitly with the text. Hereticus 2:27, for example, has obviously gotten misplaced.

THE GOSPEL ACCORDING TO ST. HERETICUS

Chapter 2

[1] Once upon a time God lived at the North Pole. He wanted little boys and girls to be happy and have lots of good times. But if they wanted toys, they had to be good. [2] So God sent a spaceman to tell the shepherds not to be afraid, because even though Santa Claus was coming to town, Herod was going to kill all the little babies. Next

week on the ABC television network the three wisemen watched the baby Jesus coming to earth [3] in a spaceship that was so bright it looked like a star. [4] They followed the spaceship for a long time. But they didn't get tired, because they came in a sled that was drawn by three camels named Prancer and Donder and Blitzen, and the sled went jingle, jingle, jingle, all the way. [5] The noise frightened the shepherds' sheep, who started to run, and the pilot leaned out of the spaceship [6] to tell the shepherds not to spank their sheep, because this would make them sore afraid.

He said that if they went to the Bethlehem Steel Company, they could see Jesus in a manger with an electric light bulb in it to keep the baby from getting cold. [7] But the baby in the manger was only a doll, so it didn't matter.

[8] The kings finally got there and had presents for the baby. One had some gold from Fort Knox, and another king named Frank Incense gave Jesus "murr," or something. [9] The shepherds didn't see the spacemen anymore, [10] but they decked the hall where Jesus was with boughs of holly, so that if bad Herod went there, he would prick his finger and die.

[11] But Santa Claus got down the chimney before Herod had a dream, and left a bowlful of jelly for Mary and Joseph, because they couldn't get into the hotel for supper. [12] Mary was great with child, so she was the baby-sitter while Joseph went to the garage and got the donkey. [13] Then they took a trip to the desert so Jesus could play with the sand toys Santa Claus had left, and then Santa Claus gave them a ride over the Red Sea in his sleigh [14] so that the Egyptians wouldn't drown them.

[15] Then God went back to the North Pole [16] until next Christmas and took off his red suit [17] and made more toys. [18] But it's always Christmas for Dad if he gets a carton of filter cigarettes that draw better than all other leading brands. [19] Impartial tests show. [20] And the shepherds were

late getting back to their flocks, because they were keeping their watch by night and couldn't see what time it said. But they left a special message for us [21] about telling Mom to go down to the friendly neighborhood grocer and buy a giant economy size box of Zuz, with a plastic wind-up angel inside absolutely free, [22] complete with launching platform.

[23] Since Jesus gave presents to all the animals, we ought to give presents [24] even to our aunts and uncles. He liked all the animals in the manger, because they were wearing swaddling clothes to keep warm, and there was a donkey and a cow [25] and a horse and two sheep and a bear and a lion and a hippopotamus [26] and a pushmepullyou, and all the people wore clothes made from old living room curtains.

[27] Herod's other name was Scrooge.

THE NEED FOR SOME NEW ADDITIONS — II

(*A Scripture Lesson for Easter*)

I N WHAT follows I offer the Easter story as it has come to be told in the oral traditions of modern culture-religion. While some will urge that my account belongs merely to the genre of saga, folklore, tradition, or myth, others will want to insist that it is not, for all that, the less true. It should be clear, at all events, that this is not something that I have "made up." It is sober and straight-forward reporting of the various strata of twentieth-century religious insight.

Students of the *Formgeschichteschule*, who want to dis-entangle the various sources, can start from the fact that the extant version draws on at least the following sources: SS (Sunday Schools), ss (sermons by seminarians), Ss (Sunday supplements), Pp (Protestant pulpits), RC (Radio Commercials), and StSp (Sermon topics in Saturday's papers).

THE GOSPEL ACCORDING TO ST. HERETICUS

Chapter 23

[1] But on the first day of the week, toward dawn, they arose and went to the garden in convertibles, ranch wagons, and Corvettes, wearing on their persons the spices they had prepared for the occasion. [2] And behold, as the sun burst forth there was a great blast from four trumpets, drawn from the local high school marching band. And at the blast of the trumpets, an Easter bunny, wondrous large, stood before them. [3] His appearance was like lightning, and his fur was white as snow. [4] And he did carry a sign affixed to his hat bearing the words, "Courtesy of Jones's Department Store."

[5] And in great joy at his appearing, all the children began to clamor and to shout, [6] saying as with one voice, "Who will roll away the eggs for us?" [7] For at his appearance it was as though the miracle of spring had been enacted once again, and that from the belly of the Easter bunny had come forth many eggs, some green, some yellow, some chocolate; and red, white, and blue ones not a few.

And the parents were grieved and afraid for the children, that they would pick the eggs and pelt one another therewith. [9] For it was the custom in that place that on Easter Morn all believers were to dress in new raiment. And the parents were afraid not only for the children's raiment

but for their own as well, [10] for verily all those assembled
were believers and were wearing new and shining apparel
for which they had paid beyond their means, some thirty,
some sixty, and some an hundredfold.

[11] Then all with one cry took up the refrain, "Behold
the miracle of spring!" [12] And those on the left did cry
aloud, "I believe in the deep greenness of the new-grown
grass," [13] while those on the right were heard to say,
"Verily once again from out the earth hath come forth
shoots," [14] and all together raised their voices in a mighty
chorus to repeat together, "As it was in the beginning,
is now and ever shall be, world without end. Amen."

[15] But certain scoffers there were amongst them, who
from behind their reversed collars did say: [16] "Ye know
not what ye do. [17] Is this not the great miracle of the
irruption of eternity into time? [18] Know ye not that here
the eschatological moment of all the aeons is compressed
into the facticity of the concrete, specific, and unrepeat-
able?" [19] But they said unto them, "We will hear of this
another time," [20] and they turned their backs on them.
[21] Whereat the scoffers said one to another: "It is as we
have always heard. The multitudes will not gladly hear
the simple word of the gospel, for verily their ears are
enstopped by the sin of their *hubris*." [22] And they went
away content among themselves.

[23] And others there were in their midst who did speak
on this wise: "Easter is the season of joy. Be joyful in the
God of your choice, all ye lands. Serve the God of your
choice with earrings, come before his presence with new
clothes, and show yourselves glad in him with raiment and
new finery." [24] And then, with scarcely a change of intonation, the voices went on to say: [25] "For a small down pay-
ment you can own the hat of your choice with which to
worship the God of your choice. Show your faith in the
future by buying now and paying later." [26] And with one
accord they did all go forth, and he that had no money

went, bought, and did eat, and they all did sing forth praise to one another's raiment.

[27] But privily each one said to himself of the other, "Why did she buy that ghastly hat?"

[28] And some did carry placards with words of cheer inscribed thereon, for the hope and consolation of the multitudes. [29] And affixed thereto were words for the season, to wit: [30] "There Is No Death" and [31] "Make Every Day Easter Day," to which latter sign was appended in smaller letters inscribed beneath, "By Banishing All Thought of Death." [32] And one there was whose banner went, in glorious affirmation of the festival, "The Miracle of Easter Is the Miracle of Spring." [33] And many there were who carried words too small to read, but whose meaning was writ large by pictures affixed thereto, of green leaves, pansies, and new-plowed fields.

[34] And through it all none was discouraged save three. [35] And they went out and fled. For trembling and astonishment had come upon them. And they said nothing to anyone, for they were afraid.

Some of the textual critics have suggested that the MS. has broken off in the middle of a sentence. I'm willing to let it stand as it is. It seems a fit conclusion.

PART FOUR

Theology — and All That Sort of Thing

◈

THEOLOGICAL "TOM SWIFTIES"

I N MY CAMPAIGN to brighten up theological writing, I've recently come across a word game that can add zest to religious publishing for generations as yet unborn. My proposal is that we begin, perhaps quietly and un-obtrusively, to introduce "Tom Swifties" into our Biblical commentaries, church histories, systematic theologies, and books of collected sermons.

A "Tom Swifty," as most literate Americans know, is a grammatical construction in which the adverb modifying "said" (or some equivalent) is closely and preferably illuminatingly related to the preceding quotation. For example: "I'll take twelve dozen," he said grossly. Or,

"I'm sorry, I just can't see it," he retorted blindly. Or even (one about which I'm a bit dubious), "Certainly leprechauns come out at night," he replied Eire-ly.

After we've begun to plant our theological Tom Swifties we could let the advertisers in on the game: "Be the first man on your block to find the four Tom Swifties hidden in Volume I of *Either/Or*, and get the second volume absolutely free." Or: "The first five readers to identify the three Tom Swifties in our lead editorial will get a year's free subscription to *Christianity and Crisis*."

The most promising field is open to those writing Biblical commentaries, since these works of scholarship are not widely known for the spriteliness of their style. Here, then, are some starters, to get the Biblical scholars rolling on their own:

"I have sinned," said Adam originally.

"Nonsense! I'll look behind me all I please," responded Lot's wife saltily.

"But all I have is five loaves and two fishes," the Palestinian youth answered provisionally.

"I'll sit in the rear of the boat if I please," responded Paul sternly.

"I see through a glass," said Paul darkly.

But the church historians must likewise set their minds to work, and with a two-thousand-year span to work from, it should not take long to go beyond the following:

"I'm dreadfully sorry, but we're all out of wax," the Bithynian shopkeeper said sincerely.

"Well, if you really mean it, you might build some sort of monument to commemorate my victory," said Constantine archly.

"I am set right by the grace of God," Luther replied justifiedly.

The cenobite rushed out of his cave. "There's no more air in there," he gasped hermetically.

"The whole of my life, it has been shattered," muttered Pascal brokenly.

Newman excused himself. "I must go and work on my autobiography," he said apologetically.

Systematic theology, philosophy of religion, philosophical theology, and dogmatics likewise have large areas to explore:

"I'll stay here in hell as long as I like," the devil retorted hotly.

"It's nothing important," he insisted venially.

"I'm filled with the Holy Ghost," the saint replied gracefully.

"Man is on the road to perfection," the theologian said liberally.

"It's just that we see our own sins so clearly mirrored in others," John said reflectively.

"It is imperative that you reply," responded Kant categorically.

"Indeed no! Only empirically verifiable statements are meaningful," rejoined Ayer positively.

The local parish, of course, must become involved if all of this is to become relevant:

"No more pulpit thumpers," the chairman of the pastoral supply committee responded woodenly.

"I shall preach today on the reality of death," the minister announced gravely.

"But you have to make decisions in groups!" he said dynamically.

The social action people deserve one that I can't claim to have originated, and that doesn't quite follow the rules. It goes:

"But if they would just stop sending down these northern agitators, we'd work things out ourselves," Jim crowed.

There's one I still haven't been able to work around to fit the ground rules. In its present unfinished form it goes:

"But all I want to do is to call the bishops together in solemn convocation," he said in conciliar tones.

NEEDED: SOME NEW THEOLOGICAL WRITING

NOTHING seems likely to stave off the continued publication of books of theology. Although a moratorium in this area for a few decades would certainly be desirable, I'm afraid the most we can hope for is a more controlled market.

I suggest therefore that publishers, instead of waiting for authors to submit manuscripts, go out and solicit the kinds of books that are really needed, and that they go after the specific authors best qualified to write the books they want to produce.

I therefore offer below an ideal list of the books any publishing house should be seeking, and I offer it gratis in an effort to get theological writing off dead center and on the move again.

NEEDED BOOK: a readable analysis in depth of the "inner city," exploring both the sociological and theological issues with which the church must cope on this new frontier.
PROPOSED AUTHOR: St. Augustine
PROPOSED TITLE: *God of the City*

NEEDED BOOK: a biography of St. Augustine, exploring in depth his transition from a life of passion to that of a man caught up in purposes higher than his own.
PROPOSED AUTHOR: Reinhold Niebuhr
PROPOSED TITLE: *The Man of Nature and Destiny*

NEEDED BOOK: an attack in depth on linguistic analysis, urging a return to the more adequate philosophy of St. Thomas Aquinas.
PROPOSED AUTHOR: Etienne Gilson
PROPOSED TITLE: *The Medieval Spirit of Philosophy*

NEEDED BOOK: a symposium refuting in depth the philosophy of St. Thomas, written by a group of non-Thomists representative of the "modern mind."
PROPOSED AUTHORS: Randall, Russell, Reichenbach, and Royce
PROPOSED TITLE: *Gentiles Contra Summa*

NEEDED BOOK: a historical study in depth of the contribution of major Protestant groups to the development of left-wing political concern.

PROPOSED AUTHOR: H. Richard Niebuhr

PROPOSED TITLE: *The Denominational Sources of Socialism*

NEEDED BOOK: a sociological and psychological analysis in depth of the individual in the current "return to religion," describing his frequent shifts in membership from one religious group to another.

PROPOSED AUTHOR: William James

PROPOSED TITLE: *The Religion of Experienced Variety*

NEEDED BOOK: a dispassionate treatment in depth of contemporary suburban Protestant culture-religion, in which the *kērygma* (preaching) has withered away, and nothing is left but the *didachē* (teaching).

PROPOSED AUTHOR: Ernst Troeltsch

PROPOSED TITLE: *The Social Churches of the Teaching Christians* (Vol. I and Vol. II)

NEEDED BOOK: a collection of the most important articles in the theological field during the past quarter century.

PROPOSED EDITOR: Peter Berger

PROPOSED TITLE: *An Assembly of Solemn Noises*

NEEDED BOOK: a broad survey in depth of the "worship experiences" of high school young people at summer conferences in outdoor chapels, complete with charts, graphs, and other appendixes.

PROPOSED AUTHOR: William Temple

PROPOSED TITLE: *Nature: Man's God*

NEEDED BOOK: a full and extensive survey in depth of the right-wing Dutch Calvinist groups in north central Holland during the second quarter of the seventeenth century.
PROPOSED AUTHOR: Karl Barth
PROPOSED TITLE: *Dogmatic Churches* (14 vols.)

NEEDED BOOK: a broad impressionistic account in depth, from the vantage point of about A.D. 2000, of the history of Western Christendom during the previous hundred years.
PROPOSED AUTHOR: Adolf von Harnack
PROPOSED TITLE: *What Was Christianity?*

NEEDED BOOK: another best-selling life of Martin Luther, written in depth by one close to the events themselves.
PROPOSED AUTHOR: Martin Luther
PROPOSED TITLE: *The Captive Babylonian*

NEEDED BOOK: a theological analysis in depth of the contributions of existentialism, psychotherapy, modern art, and religious socialism to clear-headed vision in the foggy days ahead.
PROPOSED AUTHOR: Paul Tillich
PROPOSED TITLE: *The Courage to See*

NEEDED BOOK: a sociological report in depth on the decision of a woman's club to stamp out vice in our cities.
PROPOSED AUTHOR: John Knox
PROPOSED TITLE: *The First Blast of Women Against the Monstrous Regimen of Strumpets*

SPACE–AGE THEOLOGY

IT IS ASTONISHING how quickly heresy has been able to capitalize on the space age. Advantages are coming our way that we have not possessed since the downfall of Ptolemaic astronomy. So rampant are the possibilities, indeed, that I can suggest four points rather than my usual three.

1. "One would have thought," as the British theologians like to say before clobbering somebody, that the advent of space travel, and the unavoidable recognition that the "far reaches of the stars" really *are* far, might have served to make men more aware of their insignificant status in the scheme of things. A proper sense of humility might have been induced that would have done incalculable harm to the advancement of heresy. Fortunately, this has not proved to be the case. Not at all. For with scarcely any prompting whatsoever on our part, men have quite openly begun using the conquest of space as a vehicle for human pride. The "far reaches of the stars" are really far, they concede, but what an added tribute to us that we are in process of conquering them! At one time, they continue, man was a little lower than the angels, but before long he will be able to soar considerably higher.

So we can report that whatever awe man may once have felt before the Creator is fast disappearing in favor of self-congratulations for the created.

Clear gain.

2. But the space age presents another advantage to us.

The order of the day is surely to get men to concentrate so much on the "far reaches of the stars" that they will be deflected from concern about things close at hand. How much more exciting to contemplate being first to the moon than to worry about integrating bus terminals or achieving a satisfactory formula for nuclear disarmament! How much more romantic to speculate about theoretical people on Mars than to engage in the prosaic task of feeding actual people in Mongolia or Manhattan! Soon the real, if not consciously recognized, slogan will be, "Outer space, not inner city."

Once again, clear gain.

3. But the third advantage is the greatest of all. This is the eager appropriation by the pulpit of space-age terminology. The advantage to us is that most of the appropriation is downright silly. The first American venture into space, Commander Alan Shepard's 15-minute flight, was exquisitely timed — so much so that I'm sure some of our lads must have had a hand in it. For it came so close to Ascension Sunday that ministers all over the country were able to refer to Jesus as the *first* astronaut. Some of them went on to the comforting observation that the Palestinian's conquest of space beat the Russian's by over 1900 years, and thus Our Man was really first.

Now if this sort of thing continues, we will more than recover the losses we suffered at the hands of Copernicus. I am only waiting for the minister who tells us that the delay in the Second Coming is no cause for alarm; they're simply working out a few remaining wrinkles in the re-entry problem.

All of this may sound like mild blasphemy. It is. But the adjective is the saving factor. If the blasphemy is only mild, it is excusable. The church must surely adjust its terminology, at whatever initial scandal, if it is (in those blessed words) to Speak Relevantly.

4. Finally, there are even possibilities for the recovery of some heresies we laid on the shelf a long time ago.

How do we counter the Russian claim that Sputnik I entered outer space and didn't find God? We simply reply that Sputnik I didn't go far enough, and that God is utterly transcendent and removed from his creation. Deism redivivus.

Or, neatly switching the field, we wait for someone to point out that space is infinite. (I won't go into the intricacies of the concept of finite space; we're not aiming for the sophisticates.) Since space is infinite, God can't be "beyond" it. Very well, down deism, up pantheism. If space is infinite, and God is infinite (which, of course, he is by definition), then space and God are identical. Q.E.D. We have been in God all the time and didn't know it. Those who don't know about the fallacy of the undistributed middle will feel reassured again and stop bothering us — until they have second thoughts.

I would like to write a hymn for modern heretics to sing that would capture the new sense of salvation by space conquest. I don't know quite how it would go, save that it would express confidence that our sure hope in the space age lies with the astronauts who have already been up there. But I do have a first line.

It would be, "Shepard, like a Savior lead us."

SNARING THE SEMINARIANS,
OR CONFOUNDING THE ORTHODOX
IN THEIR OWN BAILIWICK

GET 'EM YOUNG, I say, and you can keep 'em for life (and death). Give me a child for twenty-seven years (I am more modest than Loyola) and I can guarantee to make a heretic out of him. This is one reason I have such a soft spot in my heart for theological seminaries. For what better place for the spawning of heretics than a place where orthodoxy is merely *taken for granted?*

I have found that the best way to meet the challenge of a seminary is to make sure that there are a few people around asking questions or making comments that appear to be innocent but are really loaded. Nothing, somehow, is more disturbing to the young seminarian than the inference that he is not really in the mainstream or that he is missing out on the newest thing theologically. So by planting my agents (chiefly first-year men fresh from college) in all the seminaries each fall, I ensure an annual bumper crop of heretics among the graduating seniors, and thus keep my message alive and vigorous in the church at large. These are the kinds of comments I direct them to make:

1. *To the man who knows all about Kierkegaard:* "I don't see how it's possible to make a real appraisal of Kierkegaard until somebody finishes translating the *Papiren.*" Since probably nobody ever will, this should be a useful deflating instrument for many generations.

2. *To the man who knows all about Heidegger:* "I don't read German very well . . . but I've gained the distinct impression that Heidegger has changed his mind on that matter." Notice that my lads don't even have to lie to thrust this one into the dormitory discussion. For there is no necessary connection at all between the two sides of the ellipsis. And if pressed, their instructions are simply to ask for elucidation, and not to try to "prove" a thing. The more innocently the entire maneuver is conducted, the more effective and unsettling it will be.

3. *To the man who has his New Testament theology all worked out:* "Have you ever considered what Bultmann's latest writings do to that position?" The chances are he has, and isn't a bit happy about the outcome.

If things are going a little too neatly for the New Testament expert, I have occasionally instructed my men to edge toward heresy themselves, by some such statement as, "Well, of course, that's predicated on the highly debatable assumption that Paul himself wrote Ephesians." (Alternative version: "Well, of course, that's predicated on the highly debatable assumption that Paul didn't write Ephesians.") If there are signs of consternation, a retreat can be effected by the surprised comment, "Why, I thought that was surely an open question around here."

4. *To the man who has a sophisticated theology:* "How do you mean that? Dialectically or paradoxically? It's frightfully important to know which."

5. *To the man who has some really first-rate ideas about culture, communication, etc.:* "Well, what you're saying may very well be true, in a general sort of way, *but is it Biblical?*" Here heresy is multiplied by adopting the pose of orthodoxy. The brilliant student may start to reply,

"Why, whatever has *that* got to do with it?" But he will stop and think better of it, because he will not want to create the impression that he doesn't take the Bible seriously. A doubt will have been sown, like unto a grain of mustard seed.

6. Finally, if there is no other way to deflate the promising young man in the senior class, a somewhat sneaky device is available, to be administered only *in extremis*. I tell my men to observe when a certain senior has slept until after chapel some morning. Then at lunchtime one of them is to approach him and say, his voice trembling with innocence and sincerity: "I simply couldn't make head or tail out of that sermon in chapel this morning. *What did you think of it?*" If the senior tries to bluff it through, he will be trapped in intellectual iniquity. If he admits he wasn't there, he will be trapped into an admission of spiritual iniquity. Either way, he will be trapped — in iniquity.

Maybe I don't need twenty-seven years after all.

HOW TO REMEMBER
WHAT'S WHERE IN BARTH,
OR MNEMONICS FOR MPROFESSORS

DUE to the assiduous efforts of a team of Scottish translators, the volumes of Karl Barth's *Kirchliche Dogmatik* have been pouring into the English-speaking world at the rate of two a year until finally the translators have caught up with the master. Indeed, so zealous are these hardy Scots that there was perturbation for a while lest they end up with more volumes in English than Barth had actually written in German.

Now, in a *Church Dogmatics* twelve volumes strong, with several volumes still to go, it is hard to remember what's where. And when the main volumes are broken down into "part volumes" it gets even harder. Since it is quite unrealistic to expect that English-speaking theologians are going to *read* the twelve volumes, I have worked out some memory devices by means of which professors, seminarians, and, of course, Intelligent Laymen, can remember what's where in Barth.

I/1 — In English, "one-one" means a tie; no satisfactory conclusion has been reached. I/1, therefore, is introductory and methodological, and points the way to future volumes.

I/2 — "One, two, buckle my shoe." A shoe is something on which you stand. I/2 deals with that on which the Protestant takes his stand, i.e., the authority of Scripture.

II/1 — Here we turn from nursery rhymes to mathematics. Two plus one equals three. Three equals the number of persons in the Godhead. Therefore II (plus) 1 deals with the doctrine of God.

> NOTE: Since in Barth's system the unity-in-*Trinity* is also a Trinity-in-*unity*, we find more on the doctrine of the Trinity in I/1, or I^1, i.e., one-primed, to emphasize Barth's rigorous monotheism.

II/2 — Here we resort to French, and read the volume number as "Tout? Tout!" which, roughly translated, goes, "Is everyone saved? Yes, everyone." This, then, is the volume on the doctrine of election.

> NOTE: This isn't quite fair to Barth, who is
> not a universalist. If Barth is ever hung for
> heresy, however, it won't be for espousing a
> doctrine of limited atonement.

III/1 — Easy: "Three, one, cre-a-tion." Not only
does it rhyme, but "creation" has three syllables; no
need, therefore to get confused and say, "*Two*, one,
creation," or even "*Four*, one, creation." *Three*, one,
deals with cre-a-tion.

III/2 — Here "Three" stands for God (Father, Son,
and Holy Spirit) and "Two" stands for man. (In Barth's
anthropology, "man" is understood in terms of "male"
and "female.") Thus III/2 deals with the doctrine of man
in relation to God.

III/3 — Time for another jingle. Since this volume
deals with providence, angels, the *nihil*, and all sorts of
other subjects, we say, "Three, three, *potpourri*." If you
can't remember where something goes, the chances are
it belongs in III/3.

> NOTE: Theological purists who dislike this may
> resort to the following mnemonic equation:
> III/3 = 3 × 3 = 9 = *nein* = no = nothing = the
> *nihil* or *das Nichtige*. III/3, therefore, treats
> the *nihil*, and by this time you should have
> your bearings.

III/4 — "Three, four, shut the door." This is very
specific, down-to-earth, concrete advice. And what do
we find in III/4? Very specific, down-to-earth, concrete
advice about ethical issues such as war, suicide, and
marriage. III/4, then, deals with ethics.

IV/1 — This volume deals particularly with justifica-
tion. Barth puts great stress on the cosmic victory, al-

ready achieved, by which we are justified in the sight of God. So: "Four, one, the battle's won."

IV/2 — Barth now turns to deal with sanctification, and stresses that this is a *real* possibility for all men. Our memory verse therefore goes, "Four, two, there's hope for you."

IV/3 (1) — Here is where Barth oversteps all bounds of numerical decency, by dividing the third part of the fourth volume into two halves. Our closest clue can come from quiet reflection about what should be the fate of any author who numbers a volume "Volume Four, Part Three, First Half," and be led from this to recall that IV/3 (1) gives considerable attention to "the damnation of man."

IV/3 (2) — This is large enough to be a phone number. When we hear someone say "BArth 432," we naturally reply, "Who's calling?" and the rest is easy, for IV/3 (2) is a treatment of the doctrine of the calling.

There's going to be a fifth volume. How many "part volumes" it will contain is known only to Barth and the angels, and Barth is not exactly sure himself. Since I'm not on very good terms with the angels (save the fallen ones), I think we'd better leave things where they are for the time being.

But in the meantime, on to Aquinas, and his twenty-four-volume *Summa*.

BEWARE OF BARTH

I'M HAVING second thoughts about Barth. The trouble with outlining his works is that it might actually encourage people to go and read them. And although he may, of course, turn out to be the grandest heretic of them all, who can tell for sure? The system isn't yet finished. In the meantime, however, he is certainly out to nail the rest of the heretics, and at this point I have a vested interest. Tit for tat, I say.

The trouble, however, is that I can't really cope with him on the basis of his own thought. The most I can do is to trade punches under the table and attack him at the one point of his obvious and almost total vulnerability — his verbosity. For if potential readers could be scared away from Barth on grounds of the difficulties of his style, then nobody would be forced to refute him or support him or do anything at all about him. And those of us on the fringes of the faith could continue our life unhampered by real challenge.

Here, then, is a handy pocket-size caricature of what can occasionally be found within the over six million words thus far committed to print. And my hope is that it will persuade people that the whole business is just like this. For then I can relax.

It is undeniably and indeed unequivocally a question whereof first of all basically and as such, as a proper and indeed a very necessary prius for all further investigation, without regard for any self-surrounding limitations and wholly apart from the usual perfunctory concessions offered to the so-called and self-consciously styled neo-Protestant school, we take it in hand as our major and only concern — leaving until a later time (cf. *C.D.* VI/5, para. 387) which will be more proper and fitting as such for the purposes of our investigation to deal with possible objections — to assert in the most undeniable fashion that we have to do here and finally everywhere and therefore at no other point whatsoever with the one significant action in itself and as such of the one *Deus* in and of Himself as He is. At the selfsame moment and in the same breath as we make this assertion, we must assert with all possible emphasis and vigor a corollary, a second fact, which by its very nature is not in itself a second fact as such at all, but by very nature of being a "fact" at all is indeed finally and without possibility of compromise a first fact as well, and a first fact which by virtue of its "secondness" is in truth both before and after that which it precedes and follows, to the effect (a matter to which utmost concern must be given at the proper place) that the one significant action in itself and as such of the one *Deus* in and of Himself as He is by token of that very fact that it is such and such an act of such and such a *Deus*, not fully understood as the one significant action in itself and as such of the one *Deus* in and of Himself as He is, but similarly and essentially and without the remotest possibility of distinction apart from refusing to take with any remaining seriousness the discipline of exegesis, also in the very same breath the wholly insignificant action apart from itself of man in the fullness of his separation from the threefold unitary *Deus* from whom in truth he cannot be separated but is now separated at precisely the point of his final reunion, which has never indeed from the creation of the world been anything but an assured fact beyond the possibility of man to grasp for himself, in himself, and with himself, intrinsically and as such.

G. Adolphus, Schrenk, the elder Umlaut, W. Pauck, and A. Stevenson all err in their various ways (for what follows, see *Th. Ex. H.*, VIII, 19) in failing to take with full seriousness the implications of this basic and irrevocable distinction. Their failure to do so, proceeding from what may seem to have been desirable and even necessary reasons at the time, is in large part and almost without significant exception in itself and as such responsible for the fact that t h e o l o g y is where it is today, that theology is w h e r e it is today, and that theology is where it is t o d a y. (We will develop this threefold distinction, which is the key to a true understanding of the strange movements of thought which circulate today under the name of "contemporaneous theology," as a part of our discussion of the anthropological considerations which underlie our refusal to take anthropological considerations with any full and final seriousness in and of themselves and as such.) *Credent quia non absurdum est!* Herein lies the possibility and the necessity for the true understanding of where the nineteenth century was unconsciously leading itself by failing to assume significant responsibility for any major direction of even a minor sort.

Let us now concern ourselves with an elaboration of each of these two basic points in turn, beginning in preliminary fashion with the corollary and postponing for the time being a full treatment of the prius.

PART FIVE

*The Intellectual Diary of a Collegiate WASP**

❦

THE INTELLECTUAL DIARY OF A COLLEGIATE WASP

FRESHMAN YEAR

Arrived at State U for freshman orientation. Eager to use these next four years to "clarify life goals" (cf. opening speech of Dean of Men).

Went to opening chapel service. Decided to shed chapel for next four years in order to develop own point of view, though will resume church attendance when have family.

Signed up for course in logic. Discovered logical positivism on first day. Shed belief in God but still retain belief in power of man's reasoning capacities.

Read *Lord of the Flies* for freshman English. Shed belief in power of man's reasoning capacities, but still

---

* White Anglo-Saxon Protestant

believe in psychoanalysis, which could have saved them all (as our English prof so well put it).

Finished introductory psych. Not sure whether am Freudian, neo-Freudian, Jungian, neo-Jungian, Adlerian, neo-Adlerian, or disciple of Harry Stack Sullivan.

Shed psychoanalysis. Embraced mysticism.

Spent entire weekend studying Zen Buddhism. Nothing happened, so shed mysticism.

Spent three days working out new world religion appropriating best from each existing religion. Surprised no one ever thought of this before. Explained new religion to roommate, who couldn't accept belief in All-Cohesive Source of Reality. Shed world religion idea.

Reread *Catcher in the Rye* for ninth time. Rediscovered phonies. Realize to my relief that everybody in dorm is a phony, that parents haven't got a clue what I've been through in last ten years, etc. Wrote freshman theme on ducks in Central Park.

Finished course in physics. Shed causation and determinism but recovered belief in power of man's reasoning capacities.

Sophomore Year

No recollection of sophomore year, save for discovery of moral relativism. Shed everything else. Got very tired.

Junior Year (Fall Semester)

Took course in French literature. Discovered Camus. Now believe in the Absurd. Am on abyss of nothingness.

Shed abyss of nothingness temporarily to exchange tweed sport jacket for ticket to fall dance.

Fall dance a flop. Back on abyss of nothingness. Ready for the leap.

Affirmed meaninglessness of existence in term paper. Got "A-minus" and comment, "Well-organized paper." Still getting ready for the leap.

Leaped into the arms of Faith. Faith Moriarity only girl in entire junior class who really understands me. Shed fraternity pin.

Junior Year (Spring Semester)

Have become socially conscious. Signed petition urging UN employ economic sanctions against South Africa for its handling of race problem. Have publicly stated will not drink South African sherry until they repeal race laws. Also signed petition urging right of Negroes in Alabama to live in white sections of cities.

Weekend spoiled by long fraternity meeting. Pinkos in sophomore class urged we go local because national office insists on retaining discriminatory clause in charter. Argued we should abide by wisdom of more mature minds in national office. Have nothing against Negroes, Jews, and Orientals, but feel person should be allowed to choose who he is going to live with.

As result of fraternity wrangle, have gotten new vision of American Way of Life. Busy writing term paper on best way to export American Way of Life to uncommitted nations. Glad to find something I believe in 100 percent.

Read James Baldwin. Shed American Way of Life.

Spent weekend with family. Expounded James Baldwin. Listened to reactions of father's friends. Shed James Baldwin.

Senior Year (Fall)

Engaged. Ready to lick the world. Adopted optimistic evolutionism. Nothing too hard to tackle. Can't wait to get out of here and start in.

Senior Year (Winter)

Realized big job decision lies ahead. What has education prepared me for? Amalgamated E representative says big field for refrigerator salesmen in tropics, chance to travel, see world, make contacts, get ahead, export American Way of Life. O.K., except don't like tropics. In fact, don't like Amalgamated E.

Senior Year (Spring)

Engagement broken. Crushed. Shed optimistic evolutionism. Affirmed tragic sense of life (cf. Unamuno paperback). In defiant gesture of despair, knocked over cup of coffee in Student Union which spilled on freshman co-ed.

Senior Year (Spring: Ten Minutes Later)

Have date for spring dance with cute, if coffee-stained, freshman co-ed. Shed tragic sense of life (cf. Unamuno paperback). Resumed optimistic evolutionism.

Senior Year (Spring: Ten Days Later)

Have finally made firm decision about future. Feel after one more year of thinking, things ought to fall into place, particularly through employment of power of man's reasoning capacities. Therefore have appointment with Dean to discuss possibility of graduate work.

PART SIX

Poetic Potpourri of a Priestly Peripatetic

❧

SOMETHING FOR EVERYBODY

What Goes for All the Adams Goes for All the Atoms

> The lowly atom used to be
> All of a single piece,
> Till man solved its complexity
> And threatened his decease.
>
> These words are writ across the weather
> Rent by atomic thunder:
> "What God hath joined together
> Let no man put asunder."

❧

The Little Lesson Church History Teaches Us All

> The power of hell is strongest where
> The odor of sanctity fills the air.

104

The National Council of the Churches
of Christ in America

Oh, the NCCCA
Gets bigger every day
Should this become its inspiration,
We'll need another Reformation.

~°~

The Kingdom of God in Geneva

The theocratic state
Which Calvin helped inaugurate
Was sometimes something less than that,
For Calvin was an autocrat.

~°~

Reflections on a Supposed Cure
for Church Bickerings

ONE SIDE:

Churchly animosities
Vanish while you're on your knees.
Unpleasant fights in church today
Can never start while people pray.

THE OTHER SIDE:

The prayer to love your en-em-y
Gets lost when you unbend-the-knee
And sometimes when you rise up straight
You've thought of better ways to hate.

THE MORAL:

When piety seems full ablaze
Beware of damning with faint prays.

The Peasants' Revolt of 1525

The views of Martin Luther
Would not please Walter Reuther.

❧

Unguarded Thought of a World Council Official Antici-
pating Possible Difficulties at the Next Assembly

We hope 'n'
Pray
Communion may
Be op'n.

❧

St. Augustine's Teens

(Censored)

❧

Reflections After Digesting the Six Million
Words of the Kirchliche Dogmatik

A Swiss theologian named Barth
Decries any man-centered starth.
His twelve-volume system
(In case you have missed him)
Is unlike that of René Descarth.

❧

The Baptist Influence in Ecumenical Circles

Some modern churchmen spend their time
(With diff'ring degrees of exertion)
Debating on whether the Bible stands
For partial or total immersion.

~~~

The Proposition to Which the Endeavors of the Thomists Are Firmly Anchored

Aquinas?
Timeless!
His synthesis
Convinceth us.

~~~

On Varieties of Existentialism

Jean-Paul Sartre
Upset the apple-cartre
Of Kierkegaard's contention
Re life's divine dimension.

~~~

Hollywood Rediscovers the Early Church

THE FACT:

> Movies about a Christian hero
> Getting burned by a Roman Nero,
> Seem to be held in increasing esteem,
> Especially so on a wide-angle screen.

A REFLECTION UPON THE FACT:

> The appeal of the films
> Does not inspire
> Modern Christians
> To brave the fire.

A Note on Certain Christians with "Good Taste"

> Some Christians would prefer
> The penitentiary,
> To singing hymns which date
> From the nineteenth century.

Extra Ecclesiam (Nostram) Nulla Salus

"We worship God in different ways,"
A layman says, intent to please;
"It matters not what forms we use,
So long as we are on our knees."
A haughty cleric makes reply
In unctuous words which go like this:

"You worship Him in your way,
I'll worship Him in His."

~·~

In the Pew

I wonder if the Yankees lost;
I haven't heard the scores yet —
It's bound to be noon before I know,
Praise God from whom all blessings flow;

I've doubled my sales and cut my cost;
The merger's nearly set —
I've got the data, I've got the dough,
Praise him, all creatures here below;

The party was a great delight,
(The way the punch flowed freely,
The way the cook had done the roast . . .),
Praise him above, ye heavenly host:

The market's up, my future's bright,
I'm riding high, and really,
I've done it all, it's not a boast,
Praise Father, Son, and Holy Ghost.

~·~

Footnote on Orthodoxy

Creedal rigor of a certain sort is
Closely akin to *rigor mortis.*

After a Forty-Minute Presbyterian Sermon

He preached about election
With meticulous precision.
His lucid apperception
Relieves us of decision.
The choice is made in manner bald,
We clearly are the leaven,
The saintly ones whom God has called,
The presbyters of heaven.

The preacher takes so long to tell,
The heaven he speaks of seems like hell.

✌

Notes Toward the Recovering of a Long-Forgotten Emphasis

In Protestant churches
There's been a dearth
Of living as "strangers
and pilgrims on earth."

✌

Hollywood Continues to Rediscover the Early Church but Draws Back

**FILM ABOUT JESUS
POSTPONED BY FOX**
*Multimillion-Dollar "Greatest
Story" Is Off Indefinitely*

Twentieth Century-Fox has "indefinitely postponed" its contemplated multimillion-dollar produc-
tion of "The Greatest Story Ever Told," Spyros P.

Skouras, president of the company, said last night.

The film had been cited by Mr. Skouras as one of the three major productions calculated to return the trouble-beset company to a profitable basis. . . . Mr. Skouras declined to give any reasons for the postponement.

— *The New York Times.*

"Film About Jesus Postponed by Fox,"
Twentieth, Twentieth Century-Fox,
Are you overly fearful of critical knocks
If you photograph the First Century-Fox?

"Film About Jesus Postponed by Fox,"
Spyros P. Skouras eventually talks
But offers no reasons to cushion the shocks
We feel when we learn of postponement by Fox.

"Film About Jesus Postponed by Fox,"
Can't mammon and God help Fox *out* of the box
Of the stern, disapproving investor who knocks
The financial insolvency present at Fox?

"Film About Jesus Postponed by Fox,"
"Cause for rejoicing . . ." — *Catholica Vox.*
For crosses and profits, the true critic mocks,
Do not go together — not even for Fox.

"Film About Jesus Postponed by Fox,"
A note of good cheer for Episcopal talks,

For Lutheran and Baptist and Methodist flocks,
In spite of its adverse effect on Fox' stocks.

"Film About Jesus Postponed by Fox,"
The faith is still safe from their scriptwriters' talks,
Until we are given that worst of all shocks:
"Film About Jesus Completed by Fox."

A THEOLOGICAL MOTHER GOOSE

On Stealing Bravely that Grace May Abound

Tom, Tom, the piper's son,
Stole a stole from a clergyman,
The clergyman with Tom did plead
His stolen stole he still did need.

Tom, Tom, the piper's son,
Gave the stole to the clergyman,
The parson put it on — and then
Worship could resume again.

Moral:

Are dossal cloth and sweet incense,
Rubric and appurtenance,
Miter, cassock, bishop's rod,
Greater than the Word of God?

The Return to Religion: A Plea for Self-examination

Little Boy Blue, come blow your horn,
The churches are crowded, the Sunday schools swarm . . . .
How will it stand when to heaven we mount
And Gabriel's horn calls us all to account?

The Augustinian Blues

Ba, ba, black sheep,
Have you any will?
Yes, sir, no, sir,
I can't tell.

Won by my Master,
I'm in the church,
While the *massa damnata*
Is left in the lurch.

Neoorthodox Notation

Jack be nimble,
Jack look out;
The devil's trying
To put you to rout.

Jack be nimble,
Jack take care;
Evil assumes
A deceptive air.

When Human praise
Your actions reap,
Beware of the wolf
Dressed like a sheep.

So Jack be nimble,
Your pride erase;
Salvation comes
As a gift of grace.

~ ; ~

The Kingdom of God in Our Generation

Old Mother Hubbard
Has a full cupboard;
No need for her to be wailing.
The social gospel
Has made it all poss'ble,
With proximate justice prevailing.

~ ; ~

A REVISED HYMNARY

I'M WORKING on a new hymnal. I'm going to keep the old tunes (*grand* old tunes, all of them) and simply supply new words for people who feel uncomfortable or hypocritical singing the old words. The words in *my* hymnal will reflect what people are actually thinking when they raise their voices of a Sunday morning.

The following offerings, then, are at least descriptively true. I won't go into any detailed defense of their literary merit.

Backward, Christian Soldiers

Like a fleeing army
Moves the Church of God;
Brother treads on brother,
Grinds him in the sod.
We are not united,
Lots of bodies we:
One lacks faith, another hope,
And all lack charity.

Chorus:

Backward, Christian soldiers,
Waging fruitless wars,
Breaking out in schisms
That our God deplores.

Some of the hymns need to have alternate versions to be used as local circumstances dictate:

Faith of Our Fathers, Wholly Faith

1. LIBERAL VERSION:

Faith of our fathers, once so great,
We must revise or be out of date,
We must distinguish *kērygma* from myth,
Or they won't be worth bothering with.

CHORUS:

> Faith of our fathers we accept
> (Save for the parts that we reject).

2. ORTHODOX VERSION:

> Faith of our fathers, keep it intact!
> They wrote it down precisely exact.
> Change no expression, no phrases delete,
> Their propositions cannot be beat.

CHORUS:

> Faith of our fathers, keep it pure,
> Relevance is a sinful lure.

3. AMERICAN VERSION:

> Faith of our founding fathers! We
> Now can express with clarity:
> "God's on our side, he'll hear every plea
> If we'll expand our economy."

CHORUS:

> Faith of our founding fathers! There
> Is nothing quite like *laissez-faire*.

Surely there should be a hymn showing where we place our trust in these dark days:

When Missiles Gild the Skies

When missiles gild the skies,
My heart awakening cries:
"May atom bombs be praised!"
Alight from here to there!
Make enemies despair!
"May atom bombs be praised!"

Our plan was all rehearsed
(Except They dropped one first)
"May atom bombs be praised!"
When military facts
Suggested sneak attacks,
Then atom bombs were praised.

(A short pause after which the final verse should be sung
fortissimo)

Sing now, eternal choir,
In uncelestial fire,
"May atom bombs be praised!"
They ended human war,
And man forever more,
"May atom bombs be praised!"

And then, in a quiet mood for eventide, a hymn of
penitence:

Tell Us, Canon

O God, I'm really not a cad,
The things I do are not so bad,
My actions on the whole are right,
All praise to Thee, my God, this night,

My tiny sins thou canst pass by,
The spiteful word, the little lie,
And then I can give thanks aright,
For all the blessings of the light;

My peccadilloes are so few
Compared to what my neighbors do.
From their misdeeds (such frightful things!)
Keep me, O keep me, King of Kings,

And since they much more need thine aid
Than I, thy servant undismayed,
Please concentrate on bigger things
Beneath thine own almighty wings.

                                        Amen.

Appendixes

THEOLOGICAL   GAMESMANSHIP–I — THEOLOGICAL
GAMESMANSHIP–II — THEOLOGICAL   RESEARCHMAN-
SHIP

NOTE: Copies of books by the British author
Stephen Potter, Esq., entitled *Gamesmanship*,
Lifesmanship, and *One-Upmanship* (Holt, Rine-
hart and Winston, Inc.) should be on every
theologian's shelf, since they are among the
most acute exploitations of the fact of original
sin that have ever appeared in print. Mr. Potter
applies the universal human desire to be on top,
or "one up," to almost every field of human
activity. He has not yet, however, begun to do
justice to the theologians, and the following
essays are modest attempts to fill this lacuna.

The first two appendixes appear substan-
tially as they originally did in *Religion in Life*,
being updated at only a few minor points. The
reader is invited to test his ability as a Gamesman by noting the degree of ease with which
he can update, for example, the special section
"On Not Having Been to Evanston." "Theological Researchmanship" appears here for
the first time.

THEOLOGICAL GAMESMANSHIP — I

*How to Win a Theological Discussion Without Knowing
Anything, or The Art of Using Imaginary Lances
to Demolish Real Windmills* [1]

FEW THEOLOGIANS, save the Men At The Top, really
know as much as they need to know, or, more important, as much as they need to give the impression of
knowing. If they are fully informed on the history of
Tischendorff's second visit in quest of the Codex Sinaiti-
cus, or the extant correspondence between Zwingli and
the Burgermaster of Dort, it is usually because this was
the field of their doctoral dissertation twenty years ago.

And yet daily in the classroom, at annual meetings of
learned societies, at conferences, in informal discussions,
the theologian is expected to converse learnedly on the
most recent developments in Biblical history, patristics,
doctrine, liturgics, Oriental religion, and metaphysics,
not to mention psychology and anthropology. How to
help him? What to do when confronted by the unanswer-
able question? How to engage in a conversation about a
topic on which one is totally ignorant, and still emerge
as the most penetrating commentator? It is to deal with
such serious questions as these that the present essay is
offered.

Okay Words. Every theologian must have at his disposal certain words that can be introduced casually into
discussion in such a way as (a) to indicate general knowl-

---

[1] Frequently known as Inverse Quixote-ism.

edge, but not in such a way as (b) to elicit pinning down. The following are Okay Words for 1953: Bultmann, Lund, Tillich'sfirstvolume (one word), *Scottish Journal of Theology* (four words), nonbeing, Kierkegaardian (pronounced "Kierkegorian").

Non-Okay Words. These are to be mentioned only in disparaging terms: neoorthodoxy, natural theology, humanism, experience, Kierkegaardian (pronounced "Kierkegaardian").[2]

What to Do About Barth. The problem is two-dimensional: (1) You must know a great deal about Barth these days. (2) You don't. What to do, therefore, about Barth?

The following procedure has been tried, and is almost foolproof. Its three distinct stages can serve, cumulatively, to flatten almost any opponent.

STAGE ONE: When Opponent is learnedly discoursing about Barth, wait until there is a pause or lull in the exposition, and then say in an offhand manner, "Of course, you know he's moved way beyond that position in the as yet unpublished final volume of the *Dogmatik.*"[3] For the full strength of this gambit, it is essential that the last word be given a strong German flavor. If someone raises his eyebrows at your pronunciation, refer amusedly, in a mumbling sort of way, to "my incurable Bavarian accent."

The reference to the final volume has the tactical value

---

[2] Both lists will be revised from time to time. It will not be long, certainly no more than six months, before "Buber" is an Okay Word. [A 1964 list of Okay Words would include the following: post-Bultmannian, Heideggerian existentialism, Montini, schema, Vatican Two, amphictyony. No book about the Old Testament may any longer be published without using the latter word in a chapter title. — Ed.]

[3] It is sometimes effective to say this as an aside, in a loud voice, *to someone other than the speaker.*

that it cannot be challenged by anyone save Karl Barth and Charlotte von Kirschbaum, who are not likely to be present. It has the further advantage that it might also be true.[4] This statement alone is often enough to deflate any self-styled "Barth expert."

STAGE TWO: If Opponent, however, shows signs of rallying rather than retreating, say quickly, after an almost imperceptible pause, and with the suggestion of a sigh, "How I wish he'd get the thing finished, once and for all!" implying that you have been pressuring him, in this direction, fruitlessly, ever since you left Basel. If Opponent is by now not completely silenced, say (Stage Three) to the most distinguished member of the group, "It would avoid so much misunderstanding of Barth's *real* position."

This series of statements will work against all theologians except those named T. F. Torrance.

The Appeal to Ignorance. The object here is to make Opponent feel either that he has made an utterly trivial theological distinction or that he is, in a rather gross way, trying to display intellectual superiority. Thus:

> OPPONENT: But you must recall Anselm's distinction between —
>
> SELF (*interrupting*): I can honestly say that I have never read a single line in Anselm that had the remotest connection with the subject under discussion. (*This is probably true.*)

Opponent either has to shift gears (a victory for you) or go into such a minute explanation of Anselm that he will

---

[4] As a general, though by no means universal, rule, truthfulness in Theological Gamesmanship heightens the ultimate effectiveness of any statement.

be hopelessly enmeshed in his own dialectic within thirty seconds.

Should he, foolish man, attempt to explain the Anselmic distinction to you, be hopelessly grateful to him, and pathetically eager to understand. Every time he stops for breath, break in just as he finishes, "Yes, yes, go on . . . ," particularly if he stops for breath only about once every ten minutes.[5] If this fails to confuse Opponent, produce a small notebook from your inside coat pocket,[6] and *take notes as he talks*, being careful to question him on his own phraseology, and also asking for specific references to Anselm's untranslated works.

The Appeal to History. Almost anyone can be put in his place by the suggestion that he is saying nothing new or is, at best, only reaffirming some ancient heresy.

> OPPONENT: Don't you think we're giving too little attention to spiritual things these days?
>
> SELF: How curious of you to say that! You are the last person I would have suspected of being a Gnostic.[7]

Other gambits are easily adapted from this basic one. In any discussion of the ministry it is usually safe to comment, in a slightly tired voice, "Surely that was all thrashed out in the Donatist controversy." Or, "I thought Cyprian had said the last word on that."

_____

[5] Okay substitute phrases for "Yes, yes, go on . . ." are (a) "Just a moment now, I'm not sure I get that," and (b) "Would you mind repeating that again more slowly?"

[6] Theological Gamesmen on the West Coast say that the vest pocket may be even more effective. Thanks here to A. Miller.

[7] In some circles it will be more effective to say, "Manichaean" or, in extreme instances, when there is plenty of time, "A type of second-century Docetist."

When discussing the Sacraments, one of two approaches (never both) is recommended. Either, "But man, that's sheer Zwinglianism!" or, "I take it, then, that you are defending magic, pure and simple." [8]

The Superior Knowledge Gambit (not for beginners). Easier to illustrate than explain:

> OPPONENT: I think my interpretation of the church has full historical precedent in Augustine.
>
> SELF (*starting hesitantly, but gradually gaining assurance until the final words are spoken with complete authority, in an* ex cathedra *tone of voice*): But surely, much as I admire your exposition, really now, which interpretation of Augustine's do you mean? There are at least five (*eyes to the ceiling for a brief moment of counting*), yes five ... (*pause, then confidentially*) There are at least five interpretations of the church in Augustine's extant writings. (*Give ever so slightly more emphasis to the word "extant."*)

It is of utmost importance that the last sentence be spoken with authority, or Opponent may be brash enough to counter, "What are they?" *Voice control* is the secret of The Superior Knowledge Gambit. Statements must always be made in such a way that to question them could only lead onlookers to infer of your Opponent: "What an utter dolt! Doesn't he *know?*" Never refer to "the Barmen Declaration," for example, in such a way that a logical rejoinder might be, "What's that?" The effect desired can be achieved either by speaking (a) passionately or,

---

[8] Oversimplifying his position in this manner is the best way to anger, and therefore fluster, Opponent. Say (genially, if possible), "Well, reduced to its bare essentials, what you are *really* saying is ..." and proceed to caricature.

sometimes, (b) offhandedly, so that the impression is conveyed that "we both know what I'm talking about."

Suppose, however, Opponent does challenge The Superior Knowledge Gambit. Only one thing to do: bluff it out as good-humoredly as possible:

> SELF: Oh, well (*shrug of shoulders*), I don't want to bore you and all these good people with a thirty-minute lecture (*chuckle*) on Augustine. Show us those pictures of your children (*playful dig in ribs*).[9]

The most foolproof use of The Superior Knowledge Gambit is actually to possess some superior knowledge and then to guide the conversation to the point where you can bring it in. See following section.

The "But Luther Said . . ." Retort. An invincible part of the armory of anyone who wants to discuss the Reformation. It consists of memorizing a few brief statements from a relatively inaccessible source such as the *Table Talk*.[10] Whenever a statement is made about the Reformation, or Luther, or the late medieval period, insert into the discussion the appropriate quotation from the *Table Talk*, prefixing it with the words, "But Luther said . . . ," emphasizing the word in this prefix which is most appropriate under the given conditions. If page number can be quoted, so much the better. It is not,

---

[9] This should be practiced several times *before a mirror*. It must convey the impression that you spent last summer visiting French abbeys collating the various Augustinian manuscripts and checking for errors in translation, but that you are really a family man at heart, with a keen sense of what is ultimately important to your Opponent.

[10] In dire emergencies it is considered *de rigueur* to quote from Roland Bainton's *most recent* book about Luther. (*Note:* British Gamesmen should substitute the name of E. Gordon Rupp.) Lists are being compiled for aid in each instance, but it is admittedly hard to keep up to date.

however, yet considered in good taste to quote the passage in German before translating it condescendingly.[11]

The Offhand Use of Foreign Words. A few of these are essential:

1. *Schöpfungsordnung.* Essential in the field of ethics. Happily for Gamesman it can be referred to either (a) with approval or (b) disparagingly.

2. *Pacem in Terris.* Convenient when referring to a papal encyclical. Thus: "As Pope John put it in — was it *Pacem in Terris?*"

3. 'Εν ἀρχῇ ἦν ὁ λόγος. To be muttered under the breath, yet audibly, whenever someone refers to the Fourth Gospel.

4. It is sometimes effective to refer to "Jean Cauvin, or, as we have come to call him, Calvin."

5. *Agapē.* This is almost an Okay Word. It must *always* be used, as the English word "love" is inappropriate to theological discussion. Stress the second syllable. It is always stylish to refer to "the Biblical notion of *agapē,*" and even more stylish to refer to "the distinctively Biblical notion of *agapē.*"

NOTE: The latter phrase, properly inflected (and it needs careful practice), is capable of starting the following chain of reason in the mind of Opponent: "This man is no fool. He knows his Greek. He has obviously read Nygren, he has mastered Kittel, he is acquainted with

---

[11] Note to Presbyterians: The "But Luther Said . . ." Retort can be effectively adapted, with a minimum of trouble, to a discussion among Reformed theologians. The procedure involves three steps:

1. For "Luther" substitute "Calvin."
2. For *Table Talk* substitute *Sermons on Job.*
3. Proceed as above.

the criticisms of Father D'Arcy, and he has probably exposed himself to the writings of Denis de Rougemont."

It is even possible to pronounce *agapē* in such a way that Opponent will instinctively be aware that you would pronounce its opposite "air-ose" instead of (vulgarly) "air-oss." One of the deepest rewards of Gamesmanship is the knowledge that such thoughts are lodging themselves inextricably in the mind of Opponent.

6. ". . . you mean you haven't studied Ugaritic?"

Palsy-Walsy With The Great. Two basic lines of approach here:

1. On-the-"in"-with-the-World-Council:

> SELF: "'t Hooft said to me just last week before he left for Geneva . . ." (*No need to point out that he also said it to 1,450 other listeners in a public auditorium in Columbus, Ohio.*)

Or,

> SELF: "Well, I've decided to pass up the next Faith and Order meetings. I rather fear I'll be knee-deep in galley proof by then . . ." (*Followed by a mumbled and deprecatory reference to ". . . publishers very insistent . . . ," said in such a way as to indicate that you are far too modest to wish to discuss your forthcoming book. This creates the impression that you have been* invited *to the Faith and Order meetings, probably by someone in Geneva who has written you, addressing you by your first name.*)

2. If by any chance you have seen a prepublication copy of a new book by a prominent theologian, remark casually, "I was looking the thing over before Scribner's put it on the market, and honestly, I

hadn't a thing to suggest." (*You are not obli-
gated, in this gambit, to add that nobody, Scribner's
particularly, asked you to suggest anything.*)

The Book Review Shortcut. There are three basic ways of
making use of book reviews:

1. Read *only* the reviews, never the books: "When I
saw how Pauck went after him, I knew he wouldn't be
worth my time." (*This is a great time-saver for busy Gamesmen.*)

2. Read *all* the reviews: "Strange, isn't it, that two
men so far apart as Wieman and Brunner should both
like Feemer's new *Symbolics*. It makes you wonder . . ."
(*voice gradually trailing off*).

3. Be *stimulated* by reviews: "I'm devoting the entire
month of January [12] to finding out whether this new thing
on von Hügel is really all that good."

*Impressing Oneself on the Group as a Person with a
Definite Position.* Discover the theological position of the
group you wish to crash, and then employ *one* of the two
following opening conversational gambits, depending on
whether you wish to evoke the response: "Ah! This
fellow is really one of us!" or, alternately, "What a
courageous chap to say a thing like that *here!*"

1. "After all, though, it's not theology that's so important, I always say. It's living that really counts."

2. "There is not a single question worth asking that
is not rooted in the necessity of affirming man's utter
impotence."

---

[12] Be sure that the month named is at least four months in the
future, to convey the feeling that, desperate as you are to confirm
your impression, every minute is absolutely blocked out until
then.

Equipped with these simple weapons in his theological arsenal, the Theological Gamesman can "sally forth to the fray" (as has been so well said by others), confident of undermining his Opponent and thus making real and fine and true the great statement by — was it Melanch- thon? — that "There is no substitute for Victory."

THEOLOGICAL GAMESMANSHIP — II

With a Special Section, "On Making the Best of Not Having Been to Evanston"

LIKE EVERY infant science, Theological Gamesmanship [1] flourishes best when many minds, after pursuing independent research, correlate their findings. The present monograph attempts no more than a bringing together of the most significant discoveries in this field since the publication of "Theological Gamesmanship — I." [2]

New Okay Words, a revised list: Buber,[3] Theinterpreters- bible, Thelibraryofchristianclassics (each one word), Kittel,[4] *Heilsgeschichte*,[5] Lesslie Newbigin,[6] Evanston.[7]

---

[1] For a definition of this phrase, cf. "Theological Gamesman- ship — I," above, subtitle.

[2] Glance back over the previous few pages.

[3] Cf. the prediction in *op. cit.* that this would be the case.

[4] Whenever the meaning of a Biblical word is discussed, ask, with some eagerness, "Did you get that from Kittel?" If, how- ever, you are persuaded by the researches of J. Barr (cf. Introduc- tion to the present volume), say disparagingly, "You probably got that from Kittel." If Kittel, either pro or con, seems like Dangerous Territory, ask of any given word, "What's its Aramaic equivalent?"

[5] Appropriate whenever such a phrase as "the drama of the

New Non-Okay Words: existentialism. It has become clear that this word is fraught with danger. Opponent can retort: "Do you mean Christian existentialism, humanistic existentialism, atheistic existentialism, ontic or meontic existentialism?" [8]

The Duns Scotus Diversion. The most exciting example of Real-Life Theological Gamesmanship that I have observed in the last year took place recently in a discussion group which I was invited to attend, and deserves rather extended analysis.

About halfway through the evening, a student who had not taken very active part in a heated discussion intervened to comment, "Personally, (*pause*) I feel sure (*pause*) that the last word on this subject, (*pause*) philosophically speaking, that is, (*pause*) was enunciated by Duns Scotus (*long pause*) with his doctrine (*pause*) of *hecceity.*" I was dazzled by the sheer daring of this maneuver, but more dazzled still by the respectful silence that followed it. [9] No one challenged the statement or asked so much as a mild, "How?" or, "In what way?"

Analyzing this gambit, I think we can attribute its success to the four following factors:

1. The statement was delivered slowly (*pause*), and deliberately, (*pause*) and therefore (*pause*) authoritatively.

Old Testament" occurs in a conversation. Then, Self: (murmuring): "Ah, yes, *Heilsgeschichte . . .*"

[6] Better written than spoken. Hard to inflect vocally so as to make clear that you know about that extra "s."

[7] As in "On Making the Best of Not Having Been To"; cf. below.

[8] Thanks here to the Rev. L. Shein, M.A., Ph.D. (Tor.), our most brilliant Gamesman north of the border.

[9] I knew for a fact that no one else in the room had ever heard of the word *hecceity.*

2. It was a statement that took considerable background to challenge.

3. It included a foreign word,[10] and an impressive one at that.

4. It included two important disclaimers, viz.: (a) "personally," and (b) "philosophically speaking, that is," making it possible in case of challenge for Gamesman to respond respectively with: (a) "I'm not at all surprised that Gilson disagrees. This is merely my own theory, on the basis of a rather rough translation I made of the *Opus Oxoniense* summer before last," and (b) "What you say may be very true, but isn't it a bit beside the point? I wasn't talking about Scotus' *theology*."

I went home and looked up the matter in question. (It took me about three hours.) Gamesman had hit the nail squarely on the head.[11]

Although there is no other conceivable situation in which this particular remark would be even remotely appropriate, it should be possible to transfer the Duns Scotus Diversion to dozens of worthwhile uses by a judicious adaptation of the four factors cited above.

Mastering the World of Books. Most of us face our gravest problem in trying to keep up with the new books. It is a fact, which too few people have had the courage to face squarely and honestly, that *no* one can keep pace with the new religious books that glut the market each month. And since it is becoming exceedingly common-

---

[10] Cf. "Theological Gamesmanship — I" above, "The Offhand Use of Foreign Words."

[11] In certain circles this fact would reduce the effectiveness of the gambit, but *in this particular case* I feel that the incidental fact that the statement was true does not materially detract from the brilliance of the maneuver.

place and even tedious [12] to dismiss pointed questions about contemporary religious literature with the statement, "I never read a book until it has had at least five years [13] to prove itself," some further devices are obviously called for, and are hereby offered:

1. *Making use of foreign titles*. Certain books achieve an international reputation before being translated into English. It is therefore impressive to *refer to them only by their foreign titles* (usually German), as a way of suggesting that you were thoroughly familiar with them long before someone undertook the essentially vulgar task of translation. A handy list is appended:

HANDY LIST OF FOREIGN BOOK TITLES

Cullmann, *Christus und die Zeit*
Spengler, *Der Untergang des Abendlandes* [14]
Barth, *Die kirchliche Dogmatik* [15]
Schleiermacher: refer to "the *Glaubenslehre*"
Augustine, *De Civitate Dei* (never, for example, *The City of God*)

NOTE: The Stumbling Translation Technique, so effective with Spengler, is fraught with danger here. To refer, for example, to "Augustine's great work, *God's City*" is to

---

[12] What might be called a Non-Okay Maneuver.

[13] With people whom one sees frequently, the figure can be doubled or quadrupled.

[14] For an unusual, and often stunning, effect, give your own rather stumbling translation of this work, perhaps *The Decay of the Occident*. This will suggest that you have lived so long with your own German copy that you have never bothered to glance at an English translation, and may, in fact, be unaware of the latter's existence.

[15] Now that all the extant volumes are in English, this becomes more and more important.

run the risk of creating an impression that you cannot distinguish between the collected writings of Augustine and those of George Williams Webber.

It is sometimes helpful to compare an original title with a translated title. Thus:

GAMESMAN: For me, the whole of theology is summarized in the title of Brunner's *Wahrheit als Begegnung*, "truth as encounter."
OPPONENT: Oh, is that a new book of Brunner's?
GAMESMAN: Dear me, no! The English translation was called — let me see — *The Divine-Human Encounter*, or some such thing. Came out about twenty years ago.

2. *Knowing the great writers by their obscure books.* Since it is usually too hard to master the mature writings of contemporary theologians, a safe way out of possible embarrassment is to become familiar with one early (and more easily digested) book by the man in question. Since this will probably be unknown to Opponent, the discussion can be shifted to ground with which Gamesman is thoroughly familiar. Thus:

GAMESMAN: Yes, certainly I've gone through *The Nature and Destiny of Man*, but actually, you know, the whole thesis is present in germinal form in Niebuhr's earlier work, *The Contribution of Religion to Social Work*. You haven't read it? Why, there's existential writing at its best! Rather hard to come across these days, I'll admit, but I have a copy I might be able to lend you for a few days. I refer to it pretty constantly.
Or,

OPPONENT: What did you think of Tillich's first volume? [16]

GAMESMAN: Oh, I know it's all the rage to be reading the *Systematic Theology* these days, but actually I've never been able to get over my enthusiasm for his little book on *The Religious Situation*. Absolutely basic for a true understanding of his position. I don't believe I'd understand Tillich at all if I hadn't given a summer to it back in '37. *What did you think of it?*

3. *The Masterful-Little-Volume Maneuver.* It is often sufficient to appear enthusiastic about a book in such a way as to suggest that although you are far too charitable to say so outright, the book, to your way of thinking, isn't very substantial. All that is involved is referring to *a really first-class book* as a "masterful little volume."

Example: "Have you seen Nygren's masterful little volume, *Agape and Eros*?"

While the adjective "masterful" sounds praiseworthy, it can be said in such a way as to imply an eager young author who has gone rather over his head, but whose head you are determined to pat for A Very Good Try. To heighten the attitude of condescension, it is necessary to combine the adjective "masterful" with the adjective "little" (as in example above). There is nothing quite so patronizing as the word "little," particularly when applied to a work that runs to over 700 pages or has been put out in a two-volume edition.[17] "While he was at it,

---

[16] This formerly Okay Word (cf. "Theological Gamesmanship — I" above), has been replaced by a new Okay Word, "Tillichssecondvolume," which in turn is to be replaced by the Super-Okay Word, "Tillichsthirdvolume."

[17] The book in example above was first published in *three* volumes, and has recently been reprinted in an edition running to 764 pages.

why didn't the man, for goodness' sake, do a thorough job?" is the impression Gamesman must seek to convey.

4. *Further devices for disposing of authors:*

a. *Of theologians who write too few books:* "Isn't the man ever going to have the courage to put something into print? He must be mighty unsure of his position."

b. *Of theologians who write too many books:* "A man who turns 'em out that fast simply can't have enough time for really serious study."

This disposes of everybody.

5. Finally, to quote book titles in *slightly inaccurate* fashion can suggest that although you have read the book you couldn't quite be bothered getting the title firmly lodged in mind. For clinical reasons I have given an example of this device in footnote 18.

"*Help from St. Augustine.*" [18] A quiet yet forceful way of demonstrating superiority when Augustine is under discussion is to pronounce his name in contrary fashion to the pronunciation of Opponent. Make a point of emphasizing the contrast, so that it will be apparent that you know you are right, and that not even for politeness' sake will you pronounce the name incorrectly as Opponent is doing. Either,

OPPONENT: . . . leading ideas in *Au*gustine.[19]

SELF: Aug*ust*ine [20] may have said that on one or two occasions, but . . .

---

[18] For this phrase, used in an entirely different context, I am indebted to R. Shinn, *Christianity and the Meaning of History;* cf. esp. pp. ix, 29, *et seq.*

[19] *Ogg*-us-teen.

[20] uh-*Gust'*n.

Or,

OPPONENT (*usually an Anglican in this case*): . . . leading ideas in Au*gus*tine.

SELF: *Au*gustine may have said that on one or two occasions, but the whole *Au*gustinian tradition, following, as I believe, the essential *Au*gustine himself . . .

In this second gambit, it is advisable to maneuver the conversation into a discussion of "the Augustinian tradition" as indicated, so that when Opponent refers to it, as he must, *without* pronouncing it "the Au*gus*tinian tradition," you can smile deprecatingly, to indicate that your point has been made.[21]

Brazening It Out. There may be occasions when even the most deft Gamesman will be outmaneuvered. It is well to be prepared for such occasions. I once wrote a friend, apologizing for not mentioning his book in an article I had written, as a means of drawing his attention to the fact that the article had been accepted by a well-known scholarly religious quarterly. He replied, unkindly, in kind:

OPPONENT: I appreciate your calling my attention to the little article [22] you did in *Theology Today*, as I might otherwise have missed a really superb piece by Butterfield. That alone was worth a year's subscription. Herb [23] hadn't told me he was working on this problem.

There was only one thing to do: Brazen It Out.

---

[21] With *sensitive* Anglicans, it will often be enough simply to raise, ever so slightly, (a) both eyebrows, and (b) the second, third, and fourth fingers of the left hand.

[22] An interesting adaptation of the Masterful-Little-Volume Technique; cf. above.

[23] Note use here of the Palsy-Walsy-With-The-Great Technique, described in "Theological Gamesmanship — I"; see above.

SELF (*ignoring the slurring inference about own article and picking up on the only possible opening*): Good heavens! Do you mean to say you didn't know Professor Butterfield [24] was working on that? Why, he and I spent a whole afternoon discussing it in the Senior Common Room at Peterhouse, two — no, it must have been three — years ago. How glad I am you have finally come across it!

SPECIAL SECTION

On Making the Best of Not Having Been to Evanston

This summer [see title page of Appendixes section above for suggestion on updating what follows — Ed.] several hundred of our fellow Americans will attend meetings of the World Council of Churches at Evanston, Illinois. It is inevitable that for the next couple of years they will occupy an enviable status, being looked upon as Experts, and Ones Who Will Be In Demand For Speeches. Interested little clusters of people will gather around them at conferences, synods, church dinners . . . .

This will put the rest of us, Those Who Weren't There, at a decided disadvantage. How can we (and this is, perhaps, the question of the hour) keep these few obnoxious people, with their "firsthand observations," their I-Was-There pontificating, and their inevitable Kodachrome slides ("See, that's the back of Bishop Berggrav's head") from dominating the scene indefinitely?

---

[24] Note here the rejection, temporarily, of the Palsy-Walsy-With-The-Great Technique, as a means of Putting Opponent In His Place, since it becomes obvious from the rest of the statement that Self knows the man in question well, and yet admires him far too much to apply to him the monosyllabic epithet, "Herb."

Note: It is unnecessary to give advice to delegates actually *going* to Evanston, since the question of how to behave at a Conference has been the subject of an exhaustive monograph by H. Smith, "Notes on Conferencemanship," *motive*, December, 1953, pp. 34–38.

To these suggestive comments, however, one more might be added. It will often be desirable at Evanston not to appear to be an American, since much of the rest of the theological world regards American churchmen as Shallow by definition. It is always possible to pass for a British Theologian (A Cut Above the American, by definition) by means of the following devices:

1. Keep your mouth shut. (Few Britishers sound as though they came from Kansas or western Pennsylvania.)
2. Drink tea at 4 P.M. every afternoon. If you are in a committee meeting at 4 and can't do this, either (a) leave or (b) act restless.
3. Carry with you at all times, with its title showing, a paperback murder mystery, preferably *The Case of the Fan Dancer's Horse.*
4. Refuse on all occasions to wear an identification tag.

Device No. 3 can be relied upon, even if the others fail.

Months of pre-Evanston research have shown that the following gambits are most likely to be effective:

1. *Giving the impression that you were there too.* With a certain amount of daring (and this is not a device for the timid), it is possible, without actually lying, to create the impression that you were at Evanston too. Say casually, from time to time next fall, "When I was at Evanston . . ." and follow up (perhaps after a reminiscent pause)

with such a remark as, "It occurred to me that the ecumenical movement was at last a reality — *really*, I mean."

All that is necessary to lend the strictest verisimilitude to this statement is for you, sometime during the summer, to drive to "Evanston" and think the thought, perhaps while the oil is being changed. For the convenience of Gamesmen, a list is here appended of the "Evanstons" in the United States:

> Evanston, Wyoming
> Evanston, Indiana
> Evanston, Mississippi
> Evanston, Illinois [25]
> Evanston, Pennsylvania.

The parish minister, for example, will find it well worth his while to detour fifty miles during his summer vacation so that he can in all truth make some variant of the suggested statement at a meeting of the Women's Guild next October. [26]

2. *Confining Oneself to Highly Generalized Remarks.* When asked to make a specific comment next fall about a part of the Evanston findings or to talk on the implications of one of the section reports (which you haven't read), it is possible to pose as an Expert by making a very

---

[25] For those who prefer to have their cake and eat it too.

[26] This technique, known also as Illegitimate Geographical Inference, is helpful in other situations as well. For years I have been able to create a slight stir by remarking apologetically, "In all the time I spent at Cambridge, I'm ashamed to say I never once heard C. H. Dodd lecture."

I have, I suppose, spent an aggregate of several weeks of my life in Cambridge, Massachusetts, but as far as I know, C. H. Dodd, who was Norris-Hulse Professor at Cambridge University, in Cambridge, England, has never set foot there.

simple statement and then developing its ramifications at great length, viz.: "The most significant thing about Evanston is that it *occurred*." [27]

Similar statements which may also be used, often within five minutes of each other, are:

a. Ecumenical interchange is *always* significant, even if no conclusions are reached.
b. I'm sure that the fact that things were *said*, and said *openly*, is far more important than *what* was said.
c. Personally, I'm not worried by these supposed differences of opinion. After all, if we agreed about everything, it would be time for another Reformation.
d. What a pity Barth wasn't there!

3. *The outright declaration of war:* "Was I at Evanston? Heavens, no! I'm far too busy for that sort of thing."

4. *Making things uncomfortable for the Person Who Was There.* All in all, the safest and surest line of attack, and the one on which we shall concentrate during the remaining pages. Simply play the part of The Outsider Who Wants To Know What It Was Like. There are three ways to adapt this approach to the discomfiture of Evanstonian.

First, *The Now-YOU-Tell-Us! Attack.* Thus:

GAMESMAN (*to another member of the group*): I really can't answer that question. But look — (*turning to fix Evanstonian with a steady and frightening stare*) *you* were at Evanston. Now YOU tell us! Just what, precisely, were

---

[27] In certain areas of the country local mores may dictate that the italicized word be removed, and the italicized words "*took place*" be substituted. This is legitimate.

the points of difference between the two factions in the group on "The Responsible Society"? [28]

EVANSTONIAN: Well, I — as a matter of fact, I didn't — That is to say —

GAMESMAN (*warming up*): Come, come now. Don't be bashful, man. We want to know!

EVANSTONIAN (*stalling in a way that is already obvious*): Uh, Section what-did-you-say?

GAMESMAN (*having carefully memorized this beforehand*): Oh, come, you know. The preparatory report, all we poor fellows had a chance to see, was on "The Responsible Society in a World Perspective." You *must* have read it. In *The Ecumenical Review* for October of '53. Come now, enlighten us!

EVANSTONIAN: What was your question again?

Second, *The Dashed-Hopes Decoy.* A bit more subtle. Thus:

GAMESMAN: Was 't Hooft pretty much in evidence during the meetings of Section Two?

EVANSTONIAN (*caught off base. Somehow he wasn't expecting quite that question*): Well, I don't quite know — (*he is getting ready to say, "You see, I wasn't in that section," when . . .*).

GAMESMAN (*interrupting quickly, smoothly, and innocently*): Oh, I say, I *beg* your pardon. I'd been under the impression that you were out at Evanston yourself . . . . Sorry.

EVANSTONIAN: I was, but —

GAMESMAN (*softly, but with a shade of concern in his voice*): Oh! (*turns disappointedly away*).

---

[28] If possible, choose one of the sections whose meetings you know Evanstonian did not attend.

In three simple moves, Gamesman has managed to make Evanstonian feel that he was not only unobservant but even negligent in what he did observe. At least, the suspicion has been dimly planted in his mind, therein to grow and fester. His next speech on Evanston will be a shade less confident.

Third, *The Examination of Evanstonian's Eschatological Erudition.* Surefire. Thus:

GAMESMAN: Look now, set us straight, will you? I know you spent a whole week at Evanston, talking about nothing but eschatology. What, precisely,[29] is the argument all about?

EVANSTONIAN: Well, it's pretty complicated . . .

GAMESMAN: Yes, yes, I know, but precisely what was the difference between the Europeans and the Americans?

EVANSTONIAN: You mean . . .

GAMESMAN (*maintaining the initiative*): Yes. Exactly. Was the discussion centered on the concept of *futuristic* eschatology —

EVANSTONIAN: The first couple of days —

GAMESMAN (*just the least bit annoyed at having been interrupted*): — or did it deal chiefly with *realized* eschatology? What I want to know, and what we *all* want to know is, just precisely *how* was the term defined?

EVANSTONIAN (*girding his loins for a shaky answer*): Well —

GAMESMAN (*pressing his advantage*): Don't you agree that that's the first thing we've got to get clear on?

EVANSTONIAN: I'm not sure I follow you.

---

[29] Frequent use of the word "precisely," in asking about eschatology will be *more unnerving to Evanstonian* than any other aspect of the questioning he will face after he returns home. Never forget this fact.

GAMESMAN (*genially to the group that has been gathering during this exchange*): Well, I guess if the delegates didn't get it all ironed out, the rest of us poor chaps don't need to worry too much. (*To someone else in group*) You'd think, though, wouldn't you, that they'd have made a point to speak definitively on the theme of the conference?

Since Evanston undoubtedly *will* speak definitively, perhaps too definitively, the last remark will be interpreted, not as a slam at Evanston, but only as a faint suggestion that Evanstonian somehow found things completely over his head.

In order to make the above devices foolproof — and this can be our final word — all that needs to be done by way of prior research is to look over the Evanston agenda, and then ask about something that took place on the only afternoon of the entire week when Evanstonian went out to Wrigley Field to watch the Chicago Cubs.

THEOLOGICAL RESEARCHMANSHIP

MUCH ADMIRABLE work has been done in the field of Theological Gamesmanship since the two previous articles were offered to a famished public, but with the growing attention in recent years to foundation grants, more frequent sabbaticals, and the imperative hanging over the head of the young instructor in religion, "Publish or Parish," it is time to offer advice to those whose very livelihood, let alone professional reputation, depends upon creating the impression that they are Deep in Research, and that a Book is about to appear. The arousing of theological pique in these matters can be subsumed under three heads, for, as has so well been said by others, "All gall is divided into three parts."

I. THE PROBLEM OF NOT HAVING BEEN GRANTED A FELLOWSHIP

Every year thousands of potential researchers fill the mails with their vitae, their three letters of recommendations from someone not related to the candidate, their photographs, their proposals for research, and, most important, their estimated travel budgets.

The first rule to be observed is to keep mum about making such applications since (a) the chances are about 376 to 1 against Gamesman's being awarded one, and (b) if he does happen to defy the odds successfully, a much greater stir is created by making it necessary for faculty wives to say, "You got a Guggenheim? And you didn't even *tell* us you were applying!" Gamesman responds by staring modestly down his nose, conveying the impression that this matter of getting fellowships is pretty much an annual affair that by now is a little boring.

But most Gamesmen will not get such awards, and Gamesman must be prepared for the day when his disappointment is public knowledge. Three devices are suggested, the first having to do with Government grants, the second with grants from private foundations, and the third with the rationale consequently made necessary for spending the sabbatical at home.

1. "*I was involved in a little radical stuff back in the '30's, so I didn't even bother trying out for a Fulbright.*" This has the advantage of making any Fulbright recipient

feel just a little guilty that he wasn't more socially conscious back when it counted, and of inducing new respect for Gamesman, who was willing to sacrifice professional advancement for the sake of principles. (It is also a delicate enough matter so that there is little likelihood that probing will uncover the fact that the "radical stuff" involved speaking out against Alf Landon in the Oswego County High School Debating Contest back in the fall of 1936.)

2. "*I just missed a Guggenheim.*" This should be said in brave tones, indicating that Gamesman is quite able to cope with a Tragic Sense of Life. Its success depends upon its being interpreted by Opponent to mean, (a) "I almost got one this time, but some character from Harvard barely nosed me out because his application was written on an electric typewriter," when in reality it means, (b) "The Guggenheim awards have just been made and I didn't get one — and not at all strange, considering the fact that I didn't apply."

3. "*I decided I could get just as much solid work done right here at home where I have all my materials. Besides, it really isn't fair to uproot the kids at this stage in their education.*"

II. THE GAMBIT OF LEAST LIKELY ATTRIBUTION

The Gamesman who lets it be known that he is Engaged in Research, fellowship or no, has rich new possibilities at his disposal. He is enabled to make statements so preposterous that Opponent will not dare to question them, feeling sure that nobody would go out on such limbs if he had not, in the course of his research, run across brand-new information. Gamesman's tactic: to take the thought of a theologian and *criticize him for not possessing enough of what he already has too much of* — as handy a definition of The Gambit of Least Likely Attribution as is likely to spring to mind.

Initial reaction of Opponent will be: "That sounds completely wrong, but nobody would be fool enough to say such a thing in public if there weren't some basis for it. *He must know something I don't know.*" From this it is only a step to Opponent's deciding (in what might well become a new contribution to English prose): "Whereof one cannot speak, it is better to be silent." And to Reduce Opponent to Silence is Gamesman's Golden Dream.

Sample statements for achieving this desirable end:

1. "The only trouble with Bultmann is that he takes the New Testament far too literally."
2. "If Barth's entire system weren't actually based on a covert *analogia entis* I'd be much better able to follow him."
3. "Ferré's whole trouble, of course, is that he doesn't really give supernaturalism its due."
4. "I think Niebuhr's theology would be much more compelling if he gave more attention to the pervasiveness of human sin."
5. "Kierkegaard's impact would have been greater in his own day if he hadn't been such a slave to Hegelianism."
6. "I like Torrance's stuff very much except that I can't abide his existentialism."

III. Making the Most of the Fact that You Are Still Working on Your Ph.D.

There are occasional squares who finish their dissertations in short order and jump immediately into forty happy years of lecturing and correcting midterm quizzes.

For most Gamesmen, however, the task of Finishing the Thesis is going to be a matter of four or five summers of disagreeable, sweaty work. Even this grim necessity, however, can be parlayed into a number of advantages, most of them stemming from the fact that Gamesman, because of his involvement in research, will be "up" on all sorts of obscure data that are not so readily at the tongue-tip of Gamesman's Opponents. Three devices in particular are recommended:

1. *Language Adeptness.* In most cases, research will involve familiarity with one or more foreign languages. This temporary advantage should be pressed for all it is worth. Here, of course, is where people in the Biblical field have an unfair advantage, for in addition to the standard (a) French and (b) German, they will have to know (c) Hebrew, (d) Greek, (e) Latin (for the Vulgate), (f) Aramaic, and (g) at least one of the following: Ugaritic, Syriac, or Coptic. (See attached handy checklist for Biblical scholar's self-appraisal of language adeptness.) Therefore, the man in the Biblical field should never emphasize his thesis title or area of research when talking to non-Biblical people (other Researchmen have topics and areas), but should steer every conversation into an area where he can display his linguistic ability, e.g.: "Thank goodness, Coptic is easier than Syriac." [1] Again: "Now that I've got a year of grammar under my belt, Arabic is *really fun.*" A slightly more subtle technique is to appear ever so slightly dazed by it all, but in such a way as to convey the distinct impression that Gamesman has a lot *more* to be dazed about than Opponent has, viz.: "I used to wonder why the New Testament people put so much

---

[1] Alternate version: "Thank goodness, Syriac is easier than Coptic."

Handy Checklist for Biblical Scholar's
Self-appraisal of Language Adeptness

INSTRUCTIONS: Place an x (*x*) before each language now mastered, and an o (*o*) before each language still to be mastered. If x's outnumber the o's, Researchman is ready for initial forays into realm of displaying language adeptness.

   <u> x </u> English
   _____ French
   _____ German
   _____ Hebrew
   _____ Greek
   _____ Latin
   _____ Ugaritic *
   _____ Syriac *
   _____ Coptic *

(* One of these three is sufficient for the Junior Gamesman.)

NOTE: If the languages are placed in two parallel columns, the Handy Checklist can be reproduced on a 3 × 5 card and thus be more readily available to Gamesman for checking.

stress on Aramaic, but after three years of it I think I'm beginning to see the point." If pressed, Gamesman continues with utmost simplicity, "It absolutely illuminates Q."

The only defense against such vulgar displays of language adeptness is for the non-Biblical specialist to turn on the Biblical specialist and press the following point, with a certain puzzlement showing on his face: "See here now, you claim to be a Biblical expert. How have you managed to master your field without studying Middle Phoenician?"

It is harder to indicate language adeptness in other fields, but the church history people have certain built-in advantages:

a. "It's the untranslated stuff in Julian of Eclanum that's really exciting."

b. "I never *could* understand the developments in Augustine's thought until I read (*here the Gamesman must pronounce very carefully*) the *Retractiones.*"

c. "Medieval Latin's really not so bad . . ."

But what about the pitiable creatures (and this includes many of our most able Gamesmen) whose research is limited to English sources? They must stay in the linguistic race, and yet they can do so only by superior bluffing. The following tested examples are offered to get them warmed up for real competition:

a. "I've run across several of Niebuhr's works in Japanese. It's very hard to render the subtleties of his thought in another language."

b. "I've just discovered twelve volumes of Phillips Brooks's sermons in Dutch."

c. "Not a single book of Nels Ferré's is available in Icelandic."

Note the key to the confident use of such statements: *in no case is a knowledge of the language in question necessary in order to make the statement.* The impression, however, is created that Gamesman has (a) a fluent acquaintance with Japanese and (b) Dutch, and that he must have combed the card catalog of the Library at Reykjavík before making statement (c).

2. *The Subject-Object Inversion* (or *"Outler Agrees with Me"*). It is basic to Researchmanship that the Subject-Object Inversion be mastered, but care must be taken not to try it twice on the same person. The technique is to take a not-too-well-known and, if possible, slightly startling idea of some prominent contemporary theologian, and toss it casually into a discussion as though it were Gamesman's own idea. Someone will inevitably take issue, perhaps going so far as to hoot, and after the discussion has proceeded for some time, Gamesman says, quite casually, "Well, all I can say is that Outler agrees with me." The impression to be conveyed is that Gamesman recently had this out with Outler, once and for all, possibly at a Danforth Conference, and finally convinced him.

In a certain sense Gamesman's casual utterance will be true, but its truth will be dependent upon the practice of the Subject-Object Inversion. The statement that would be *fully* true would run: "I [subject] agree with Outler [object]." No one could deny that Gamesman might be defending an idea he had seen in a book by Outler. But no one would care. However, by inverting the subject and object, so that the statement now goes, "Outler [formerly object, but now subject] agrees with me [formerly subject, but now object]," a mild sensation can be made to occur and Gamesman will be the object of a new kind of respect.[2]

---

[2] Care must be taken that the theologian cited is living. The desired impression is simply *not* conveyed by the man who says, "Calvin agrees with me," or "Gregory of Nyssa agrees with me." Even some living theologians must be discarded from the list of possibilities for the Subject-Object Inversion, unless Gamesman

3. *Casual Use of Esoteric Information.* When asked, "What are you writing about?" Gamesman must reply in such a way as to imply that Opponent knows as much about the specialized material of the thesis dissertation as Gamesman does. Since Opponent won't, he can be made to feel inferior, a consummation devoutly to be wished. Possible responses:

a. "Oh, I'm just working on the Nam Hagadi stuff."
b. "I'm digging through the Dort material to see what I can find." [3]
c. "I'm weeding out all the *apokatastasis* stuff in Barth." Here the advantages are that Gamesman uses a foreign word [4] and also gives the impression that Barth has an untidy mind that Gamesman is about to unravel for the benefit of the nonspecialists. [5]

---

has previously established that he spent considerable time (possibly during his military service) in the country in which the theologian teaches, so that it can be inferred that he actually met and talked with the man in question. But for a man who has never been east of Cape Cod to assert, "Bultmann agrees with me," would be to be treading on very thin ice indeed.

[3] A device for hiding the obvious. If Gamesman were to say, "I'm writing on the doctrine of predestination as it was developed by the Synod of Dort and contested by Arminius," the response of Opponent would be, "Surely that's been done before." But to refer without amplification to "digging through the Dort material" is to imply that a new body of literature has just been unearthed and that Gamesman is the first scholar to have access to it. There is furthermore the possibility that Opponent will not recognize the word "Dort" (particularly if it is slurred over to sound like "Drrrt" or even "Dirt") and will think that Gamesman has access to a new manuscript dug up in the sands of Egypt by Archaeologist Diert and not yet available to the general public.

[4] *Vide supra*, "Theological Gamesmanship — I," section on "The Offhand Use of Foreign Words."

[5] Gamesman's actual title is probably quite run-of-the-mill, possibly, "A Consideration of Some of the Implications of Karl

d. A more daring maneuver: "I'm working on the anti-oedipal overtones in Augustine's *Confessions*." To say this is to be asked to say more. So, with a maximum of casualness, bordering on boredom, Gamesman continues: "Surely it's fairly obvious that since Augustine couldn't murder his father, because he was dead, he transferred the complex to his mother, and since he couldn't murder her, because he was a Christian, he took it all out on Pelagius. After all [here an increase in casualness], 'Peleg' means 'matricide' in the dialect of one of the north African tribes that used to encamp not far from Hippo."

If *every word* of this is said in tones of flat, unexcited assurance, Opponent will depart from the scene to read the *Confessions* in a new light.

Has Gamesman any defense when the above tactics are used against him by Opponent? The surest defense, of course, is *never* to ask Opponent what he is working on, since Opponent will, even by accident if not design, be bound to make use of one of the three devices suggested above. Should it happen, however, that Opponent seizes the initiative from an unwary Gamesman and gives a long, esoteric account of his research project, Gamesman has no choice but to hear him out, examine the seven-page, single-spaced, mimeographed outline very carefully, and then say, puzzledly, "But why is no attention being given

---

Barth's Doctrine of Election, as Developed in the *Church Dogmatics*, with Special Reference to the Problem of Universalism and Criticisms Thereof by H. Emil Brunner, G. C. Berkouwer, and George Hendry."

to the recent studies of Wilhelm Kamlah and Gerhard Ebeling?"

Opponent may even start to reply, "Because they have nothing to do with the thesis topic," but he will realize that such an admission would leave him Vulnerable. (Who has ever read the most recent article of either Kamlah or Ebeling?) He will therefore have to turn to a study of every recent German periodical, and until he has done that (*zwischen den Zeiten*, as the Germans say) his days, and his nights as well, will be accompanied by a vague unease.